WHAT'S the DEAL
WITH
WICCA?

WHAT'S THE DEAL WITH
WICCA?

A DEEPER LOOK INTO THE DARK SIDE OF TODAY'S WITCHCRAFT

STEVE RUSSO

BETHANY HOUSE PUBLISHERS

Minneapolis, Minnesota

Published by Bethany House Publishers
11400 Hampshire Avenue South
Bloomington, Minnesota 55438

Bethany House Publishers is a division of
Baker Publishing Group, Grand Rapids, Michigan.

Printed in the United States of America

Library of Congress Cataloging-in-Publication Data

Russo, Steve, 1953–
What's the deal with Wicca? : a deeper look into the dark side of today's witchcraft / Steve
Russo.
    p. cm.
    Summary: "Russo lays bare the spiritual roots and exposes the deception of Wicca. He
also demonstrates that Christianity is the only way to address the needs in the lives of
teenagers"—Provided by publisher.
    ISBN 0-7642-0136-0 (pbk.)
    1. Occultism—Religious aspects—Christianity. 2. Witchcraft. 3. Apologetics.
4. Teenagers—Religious life. I. Title.
    BR115.O3.R87   2005
    261.2'994—dc22   2005018444

Dedicated to

Tony, Kati, and Gabi,

Thank you for your encouragement and love.
You make my life complete and my heart smile!

STEVE RUSSO is the author of twelve books and numerous magazine articles. He is also the featured speaker of the music video TV show *24/SEVEN*, host of the daily radio feature *Real Answers*, and co-host of Focus on the Family's weekly teen talk radio show *Life on the Edge— Live!* Steve is a professional drummer and makes his home in Southern California.

TABLE OF CONTENTS

INTRODUCTION

LIFE IS SERIOUS STUFF TODAY. It's a constant flow of crises and challenges. Security is a difficult thing to find. You can't count on families; they don't always work real well. School doesn't seem very relevant, and friends are irresponsible and flaky. Unrealistic expectations are coming at you from every direction, and a balanced life seems next to impossible to achieve. What do you do? Where do you turn?

Many teenagers today are turning to the craft for answers. Teens want to know what witchcraft really involves and if it can help them find meaning in life. Whether you are already involved in Wicca, at the curiosity stage, or wanting to help a friend, this book is written for you. I want to help you sort through the confusion and find out what is really true about this earth-centered religion. But more than that, I want to give you some real answers about spirituality and your desire to make sense out of life.

I spend about twenty weeks a year speaking on public school campuses in North America. I also speak at dozens of other events for teens throughout the year, and I co-host a weekly, nationally syndicated teen talk-radio show called *Life on the Edge—Live!* In other words, I spend a lot of time with teenagers. When I'm not speaking to them, I'm listening to them. I understand your hopes and dreams, your heartaches and fears. The daily struggles with peer pressure, homework, and seemingly obnoxious teachers. And most of all I understand your need for help and answers to get through it all.

As you read these pages, know that I care about you and believe in you. In fact, I owe my life to a teenager, and I'll tell you why in chapter eleven. You're the greatest natural resource we have in the world today. Nothing is more valuable than you are. You're more precious than any amount of silver or gold or precious gems. Society's hope for the future—and the present—rests with you. You have the potential to change your world. However, if you're going to be successful and experience a life of meaning, it ultimately comes down to making the right choices. And that's why I want to do everything possible to help you handle the issues and challenges of life.

Let's face it, most kids today are curious and want to "discover" things for themselves. I don't want to force you to believe in God or anything else. Instead, I want to challenge you to *think* as you read this book. Hopefully you will come to some conclusions about life, spirituality, and Jesus on your own. And I hope that in the process you will discover for yourself the source for lasting peace, meaning, and power in life.

Steve

CHAPTER ONE

MEET THE NEW
INITIATES

I'D JUST FINISHED SPEAKING at my second high school assembly for the day, and as usual, there were a lot of students wanting to talk with me. When I talk about choices, the questions and comments from the students usually cover a variety of topics including suicide, pain, divorce, gangs, and witchcraft. This school was no different.

I noticed three students hanging back, several steps away from the rest of the crowd that was around me. Once everybody else left, they approached me.

"Thanks, Steve, for your presentation," said Emily, the short blond girl.

"Yeah," said Andrew, "we really liked what you said."

Melissa, the tall girl with short brown hair, said, "And we liked your drum playing, too. It was awesome."

"But there's one thing we want to talk with you about," said Emily. "You're not exactly right about Wicca. It's not just about power."

"Yeah," the other two added. "You're a cool guy, but we wanna help you get your facts right about Wicca."

"You gotta know this one thing, Steve," Emily went on. "We all used to be Christians, but we got turned off to being involved in church. We never found anyone there who could explain what they believed and why."

"Yeah," added Melissa, "and everyone seemed powerless, like they were already living in some kind of defeat."

"That's not how I want to spend the rest of my time on planet Earth," said Andrew.

Then, almost in unison, they said, "With Wicca we found answers and power."

Emily finished with, "I can make up my own belief system that appeals to me without anyone else telling me what I have to believe."

The bell rang, and just before they headed back to class, I told them how much I appreciated their honesty and wished that we could've had more time to discuss their Wiccan beliefs. "We do, too," they responded.

Emily, Andrew, and Melissa are convinced that they found what they needed in life when they discovered Wicca.

I meet lots of teens like Emily, Andrew, and Melissa as I travel across North America. People who are sincerely trying to make sense out of life and find a way to make it work. They want a reason to get out of bed in the morning, and they want real answers to the difficult issues of life. Let's face it, there's so much stuff coming at you in the world today—families falling apart, threats of terrorism, natural disasters, unrealistic expectations from friends—and that's just the beginning of what you deal with at school, at home, and at work every day.

Many teens are looking for answers in the supernatural. They want to tap in to the source of ultimate power to change their lives—to feel special and get the relationships they want and need. Some want power to get vengeance on people who've hurt them. Pop culture's filled with allusions to witchcraft and the occult as being the source for power and all the answers to the issues of life. The fastest-growing religion today among high school and college students is Wicca. Also known as the practice of folk magick or the magick of the people, it's a contemporary pagan religion with spiritual roots in the earliest expressions of the worship of nature. For people like Emily, Melissa, and Andrew, Wicca seems to be the ticket that gave them a form of spirituality that would provide a sense of belonging, as well as some control over their own over-whelming life circumstances. The craft, as it is frequently called, also gave them the chance to create their own religion, complete with everything in spirituality that was convenient and appealed to them—including designing their own deities.

I wish I could say that I disagree with everything Melissa, Emily, and Andrew talked about, but unfortunately I can't. It's hard today to find people who attend a Christian church and can tell you why they believe in Jesus and what the Bible actually teaches. And it's true, there are a lot of people who call themselves Christians who are living defeated lives. But maybe we need to look further than just the organized Christian church for answers as to why these things happen. Because God didn't want us to be robots, He gave us the freedom of choice. This includes what we decide about Jesus and whether we decide to live by what the Bible teaches. God's power is real and it's unlimited. We must choose to either tap into it or keep trying to do things on our own, in our own way, and with our own strength.

There are questions that keep bugging me about kids like Melissa, Emily, and Andrew. For example:

- What truths about the Christian faith have they not truly seen and experienced?
- Did they honestly compare the teachings of Jesus to what they learned from Wicca?
- Do they understand how unique the Bible is? Have they seen the historical, scientific, and archaeological evidence for its accuracy? Or how about the ancient manuscript support?

Sometimes the combination of life circumstances and curiosity causes us to do some exploring in the supernatural realm. Take Alexis, for example. Even though she attended church every week, she and a friend got involved with Wicca. Alexis was struggling with not having a father in her life. He'd abandoned her when she was only a year old, but it was becoming a bigger deal in her life the older she got. Alexis felt church had become routine and boring, and the youth leaders didn't seem all that concerned about the trauma she was going through. Plus, most of the kids in the youth group didn't act like they cared much about her anyway. She just didn't seem to fit in.

So Alexis and her friend checked out some books on Wicca from the library at school and became fascinated with everything they were reading. They thought it was cool so they started buying books and collecting other things related to the practice of Wicca. The two girls grew increasingly curious about whether the spells and other stuff they were reading about really worked. Alexis and her friend started experimenting and got scared by the things that were happening. Alexis became so fearful that she began carrying a knife to school, which resulted in her getting suspended. That was it—the end of the line for her. Alexis and her friend threw all the books and stuff they had been collecting in the trash. And even though she asked God to forgive her for what she'd done, Alexis still feels guilty.

A lot of kids today feel like the Christian church isn't relevant to their daily lives. One of the problems is that they've bought into a religious experience rather than establishing a personal relationship with God. It's awesome when you can grasp the concept of having an actual relationship with the living God—the God of all creation. That sets Christianity apart from any other religion.

Also, a lot of teens fail to really understand the resurrection power of Jesus Christ. They want answers about life and they want to be challenged to make a difference in their world—but they can't seem to find this in their churches. Some people even question if God really cares about them and what's going on in their life. They want to know where God was when their mother died of cancer or why their father lost his job and abandoned the family. One girl asked me where God was when she was gang-raped. Disappointment with God is real for a lot of kids today. Obviously, pain and suffering are part of life—but it's still hard to handle. And in some situations, we may never know the reason why we experience some of the things that we do in life.

In other situations, leaders in the church have failed miserably at making the Christian faith clear and understandable to kids in need of answers for the problems they're dealing with. The lack of practically applying the Bible to everyday life has caused many kids to search elsewhere, including witchcraft, for help and hope. Unfortunately, some leaders and Bible teachers seem to be answering all the questions that no one's asking.

Wicca's got a very positive image in our society today. It's no longer some ridiculed set of beliefs based on superstition. Instead, it's become a mainstream religious system that many see as a valid alternative to an "outdated Christian faith." There are at least five major ways in which Wicca differs from Christianity and other religions:

- worship of the goddess and god;
- reverence for the earth;
- acceptance of magick;
- acceptance of reincarnation;
- lack of proselytizing activities (trying to get someone to change their religious beliefs).[1]

Wicca and witchcraft is popping up everywhere. You can find its influence in PC games, movies, music, prime-time TV shows, cartoons, and books. The number of Web sites on Wicca is growing, and there are even classes being offered online and in some public libraries. So why is Wicca so popular, especially with teens?

For many, Wicca's promise of personal power over others and the ability to control your own life seems irresistible—even among some teens currently involved in the church. Wicca is admired for its sensitivity to the environment and is seen as the female-friendly religion in comparison to Christianity's supposedly male-dominated hierarchical system. And because Christianity is perceived as being judgmental and intolerant in today's society, it's easy to see Wicca's huge appeal. Wiccans feel like they belong without the baggage of having to look, walk, or talk a certain way. Plus, because Wicca rejects moral absolutes, a person's natural rebellious nature is appealed to. And it offers the chance to develop a personal self-styled religion. The bottom line is that Wicca offers its followers the ability to set things right on their own without having to rely on a God who doesn't seem to answer their prayers anyway.

So who's right? Emily, Andrew, and Melissa? Did Alexis and her

---

[1]Scott Cunningham, *The Truth About Witchcraft Today* (St. Paul, MN: Llewellyn Publications, 1987), 62.

friend somehow miss the point of Wicca and quit too soon? Does Christianity really offer the answers and power we need and want? How do we make sense out of life?

Wicca and Christianity both can't be right. Ultimately, you will have to decide which pathway is the right one for you to pursue. But remember to choose wisely and make sure that you honestly compare what Jesus teaches and what Wicca teaches. It's not good enough to just be sincere in your beliefs. Sincerity won't get you very far when it comes to your eternal destiny or making life work on planet Earth. Neither will it give you the power for living in a stress-filled, confusing world. Maybe you have friends who are into Wicca and you're trying to understand and help them. This book will help you to discover the truth about Wicca and its exploding popularity.

Examine the information in this book carefully. Don't be afraid to ask yourself the tough questions. Think about it logically. In the end, I hope that you'll discover the answers you're looking for to make sense out of this life and eternity.

CHAPTER TWO:

WHY WICCA?

SEVENTEEN-YEAR-OLD LAUREN ATTACHES a green candle onto a picture of a friend. In the darkened room she lights the candle and closes her eyes. Inside her mind she visualizes a glowing purple light surrounding her friend's broken arm. She chants an impassioned healing incantation, hoping her witchcraft will work quickly this time.

Do you have a broken arm that needs healing, or could you just use some practical advice in dealing with everyday life? Maybe a book described by one of the following statements promises the help you need:

Find out how the Wiccan mysteries can enhance your life.

Unlock the secrets of ancient rituals, spells, blessings, and sacred objects.

Enlist the aid of earth, air, fire, water, and other natural powers and entities.

Strange brew—discover the possibilities of notions, potions, and powers for successful spell-casting.

Learn the craft techniques for gaining love, money, health, protection, and wisdom.

When you read this kind of stuff, Wicca sounds like an exciting adventure with some pretty incredible rewards. Once considered a weird religion of default for castoffs, losers, and social misfits, Wicca is now attracting university intellectuals, the "cool" people, and quite a few kids that go to church. Wicca is the religion of witchcraft and the practice of folk magick.[1] (*Magick* distinguishes the belief in using the "universe's energy" from the practice of *magic,* the illusions performed by entertainers.) It has got big appeal with teens and is showing up everywhere in pop culture.

The more books I read about Wicca and the more I study it, the harder it becomes to define it. It's like trying to nail applesauce to the wall! You can ask ten different people about Wicca and you'll get fifty different explanations of what it is and how to practice it. No wonder it's so easy to get confused!

Whether Wiccans do it solo or with a group, Wicca is very personal in the way it's practiced. That's part of the appeal—Wiccans can pick and choose what they want to believe to come up with their own "brand" of Wicca that works right just for them. There is no one right way to practice the craft. The religion is what you make of it.[2]

Let's see if we can cut through the confusion and get a basic under-standing of what Wicca is and how it got started. We'll also look at what Wiccans believe and how it compares to Christianity.

WHAT IS WICCA?

Wicca is a complicated, contemporary religion that is often associ-ated with occultism, neopaganism, and witchcraft. If you're confused about these terms, check out the glossary in the back of the book for some definitions. Wicca, also known as witchcraft or the Craft of the Wise, is a centuries-old religion. It emphasizes worship of the earth, all living creatures, and both the god and goddess.

Does it sound a bit confusing that Wicca can be both contemporary and centuries old? Here's a brief explanation: Wicca's core beliefs are

---

[1]Scott Cunningham, *The Truth About Witchcraft Today* (St. Paul: Llewellyn Publications, 1987), 2.
[2]Silver Ravenwolf, *Teen Witch: Wicca for a New Generation* (St. Paul: Llewellyn Publications, 2000), 8.

the same today as they were centuries ago, only now they've been repackaged for the twenty-first century with a contemporary look and feel. Because Wicca is a build-as-you-go flexible belief system, it's constantly fusing together the old and the new, and it accommodates the desire of human nature to be free from restrictions and outside control.

Wiccans may be female or male, of any age or race. They may meet in groups of up to fifty or more, in cozy covens of thirteen or less, or worship the god and goddess alone. Though most speak English, they may call the deities in Spanish, French, Welsh, Swedish, Scottish Gaelic, German, Dutch, and in many other languages. As a religion, Wicca exists throughout Europe, in all fifty of the United States, in Central and South America, in Australia, Japan, and elsewhere.[3]

At the heart of Wicca is a central rule called the Rede, which says, "An ye harm none, do what ye will." (A copy of the entire poem can be found in Appendix A.) Basically, this means that witches have the total freedom to do whatever seems right to them, as long as they don't harm themselves or anyone else.[4] But this is a bit confusing. Think about it: If there are no absolutes in Wicca other than your definition and my definition, to "harm someone" could mean two different things, yet they would both be right. It doesn't make logical sense.

Wiccans believe that they create the universe in which they live; therefore, their magick will have an effect on that universe. When following the Rede, Wiccans can work whatever magick or spell they feel is necessary or appropriate. They claim they'll never use these actions to cause distress or harm to come to others in any way that those individuals would not bring on themselves, ultimately, by their own actions.

Wiccan author Gary Cantrell unpacks this idea a bit more:

> As an example of "harm none," we would never wish a speeding motorist on the highway to have an accident; but there would be nothing wrong with asking the deities to arrange for a police officer with a radar gun to appear under the next bridge. An action or spell used against a known predator or assailant would not be

---

[3]Cunningham, 4.
[4]Raymond Buckland, *Teen Witch Datebook* (St. Paul: Llewellyn Publications, 2002), 5.

designed to injure or damage that person directly; but we could cast a spell to bind the individual's own conscious thought processes so that he or she inadvertently blunders into a situation where law enforcement authorities can make an arrest. In both these examples, it would be the culprit's own stupidity that became his or her undoing. We took no action or did not work to directly injure or harm either one.[5]

The Threefold Law is another closely related rule, which teaches that anything you do will come back to you three times over. For example, if a witch casts a spell against someone, it will come back to that person with three times the power. This is the Wiccan concept of karma.

Whether someone calls himself or herself a witch, god and goddess worshiper, or a Wiccan, there are some things they have in common. To begin with, they all hope to get results by worshiping nature or using spiritual forces. But keep in mind that Wicca and Satanism is not the same thing. Most witches would say that they don't even believe in the devil or accept the concept of "absolute evil." They believe that to give evil a name is to give it power.[6] Because Wiccans say they don't believe in the devil, they get offended if anyone compares Wicca to Satanism (worshiping the devil). Nevertheless, at their very core Wicca and Satanism are the same—they both reject the truth as found in Jesus and in His Word, following the same lie that was started at the beginning of human history. Adam and Eve (see Genesis 3) also chose to disobey God and try to live without Him.

But if Wiccans don't believe in the devil, how are Wicca and Satanism alike? In the movie *Constantine,* Keanu Reeves plays a jaded private eye (John Constantine) with a knack for seeing things from a terrifyingly spiritual point of view. Angela Dodson, a skeptical policewoman played by Rachel Weisz, hires him to solve the mysterious suicide of her twin sister. While she declares, "I don't believe in the devil," Constantine insists, "Well, you should—he believes in you."

People are drawn to the craft for many reasons. Some just feel different from others, or they feel a special kinship with animals—some-

---

[5]Gary Cantrell, *Wiccan Beliefs and Practices* (St. Paul: Llewellyn Publications, 2001), 44.
[6]Ravenwolf, 8.

times stronger than what they feel with humans. Others see Wicca as powerful or glamorous. Those involved in Wicca claim to have a depth of power far greater than is apparent to the average person. This power is drawn from several sources including the All (the god and the goddess), elements, ancestors, and angels. Witches use their own power—the power of the mind—to reveal what they need. According to those involved in Wicca, everybody has the power, but most people don't use it—sometimes because they're afraid. It's from this unused power of the mind, claim Wiccans, that abilities such as clairvoyance, telekinesis, and extrasensory perception (ESP) are found. We'll talk more about power in another chapter.

A big part of the allure of Wicca is being able to choose your own deity. This is especially appealing to anyone who's become dissatisfied with the structure and practices of mainstream religions.

WHAT DO WICCANS BELIEVE?

There are a couple of things to keep in mind before we look at what Wiccans believe. First, not all witches are religious. Second, Wicca is a very individualistic and experiential religion with a lot of emphasis on personal responsibility. For example, there's no need to confess sin and receive forgiveness from an outside "authority." Instead, Wiccans are supposed to own up to their actions, admit their mistakes, and make things right wherever they can.

Most Wiccans refuse to submit to any centralized authority and are against any organized belief system. Instead, they build their own religion by mixing and matching various views and practices. Wicca, like other neopagan religions, draws heavily on experience, so truth is relative. They're convinced that the only way you can know truth is through a kind of sixth sense or feelings. There are no absolutes. (This will be discussed more in chapter 4, "The Allure of Personal Power.") But there are some basic beliefs that are held sacred by all Wiccans out of which come individual practices and traditions.

Wicca is a religion built around worship of two deities: the goddess and the god. According to Wiccan belief, before the creation of the earth, the All existed. This female spirit was all alone so she created her other half—the male spirit. And even though they were two spirits, they were one, and gave birth to the universe. They made the stars, moons, solar systems, and planets. While on the earth they made water, land, plants, animals, and people.

Wiccans believe the All is both female and male—equals—and from them came the seeds of life. The god and goddess chose the sun and the moon to remind us of their presence. The sun is the physical symbol for the god, and the moon is the physical symbol for the goddess. The goddess is the female force, that portion of the ultimate energy source that created the universe. She is all-woman, all-fertility, all-love.[7] The god is the male force, the other half of the primal divine energy acknowledged by Wiccans. He is all-man, all-fertility, all-love.[8]

Wicca is grounded in worship of the earth, which is seen as an expression of the mother goddess and her companion, the horned god. Both of these deities manifest themselves in nature. Wiccans see the earth as a living goddess who blesses us and must be nurtured and cared for in return.[9] They believe that the goddess dwells in every single thing—in trees, rocks, raindrops, and even inside of you. In many ways, Wicca is similar to the nature religions mentioned in the Bible, where many gods were worshiped and religions mixed, like the fertility religions of Canaan (1 Kings 14:22–24).[10]

Wiccans also choose the form of deity that they work with based on their personal preferences and what they want to work on. For example, if they need to attract some loving energy, they might choose to call on the Greek goddess Aphrodite. Or if they have a big exam coming up, they might invoke Sarasvati, the Hindu goddess of language and wisdom. Wiccans can choose from lots of different gods and goddesses and traditions. Naming a god is all about choosing what works for you based on the things that you identify with, relate to, like, and love. Michele Morgan, in her book *Simple Wicca*, says, "The beauty of the Wiccan path lies in the freedom to create your own personal experience of worship. No doctrine dictates who or what the god or god-

---

[7] Cunningham, 72.

[8] Ibid., 75.

[9] Michele Morgan, *Simple Wicca* (Berkeley: Conari Press, 2000), 8.

[10] Craig S. Hawkins, *Goddess Worship, Witchcraft and Neo-Paganism* (Grand Rapids: Zondervan Publishing House, 1998), 8–11.

dess must be; rather, there are ancient and symbolic descriptions of their energies, and essences. The rest is, happily, up to you. Do you desire a god who is tough or tender? Do you picture him bronze-skinned or fair? Is your goddess slender, or plump like the fruit swelling on the vine, with hair as golden as the September wheat fields?"[11] Not only do Wiccans have the complete freedom to choose whatever god they want to worship, but they work with the deities rather than beg for help from them.

When Wiccans first start practicing the craft, they are advised that deities from different cultures—Greek, Roman, Hindu, Egyptian, Buddhist, Celtic, and others—shouldn't be mixed and matched. Instead, it's recommended that a witch learn all he or she can from one pantheon, and then they can branch out and learn how deities from different systems relate to one another.

A pantheon is the collection of all the different deities from one specific culture or tradition; Wiccans are encouraged to read up on the pantheon that appeals to them, an appeal usually connected to a person's needs at a particular time. Here are a few examples of various gods from the traditions mentioned above:

Greek

Athena. The goddess of wisdom is a beautiful and serious young woman. Because she is a warrior, she wears a breastplate and helmet and carries a lance and shield.

Eros. The god of sexual attraction often carries a lyre or a bow and quiver of arrows.

Roman

Fortuna. The goddess of fortune and fate carries a rudder from a ship, a sphere, and a wheel.

Janus. The god of beginnings and the guardian of doorways can see the inside and outside of all things at the same time.

---

[11]Morgan, 30.

Hindu

Ganesha. The elephant-headed god is the overcomer of obstacles. In his four arms he carries roses, a piece of his broken tusk, a bowl, and a thorn.

Lakshmi. The goddess of fortune and beauty is golden, always beautifully dressed, and sits on a lotus blossom.

Egyptian

Hathor. The goddess of love, beauty, and pleasure is a woman with the horns of a cow.

Osiris. The god of fertility and resurrection takes the form of a mummy with the head of a living man.

Buddhist

Maitreya. The future Buddha has the form of a man holding a flower and wearing a headdress.

Quan yin. The goddess of mercy will protect you from danger. Newlyweds often pray to her for fertility.

Celtic

Ogma. The god of language and inspiration takes the form of a wise old man.

Brigid. The goddess of craftspeople, inspiration, and healing has enormous strength and can help you endure hardship.

The Days of Power—the sacred holidays that make up the Wiccan calendar—come from the earliest observances of seasons and cycles. In the craft it's called the Wheel of the Year (see Appendix C). The image of an ever-turning wheel—the constancy of change, the flow of season into season, and humankind's inseparable relationship with the earth—is symbolic of the Wiccan view of life.[12]

Wiccans celebrate these eight main holidays, or *Sabbats,* all centered on the solar cycles and occuring at the time of natural events associated

---

[12]Ibid., 44.

with the change of seasons. (These are defined and explained in the book's appendix.) At least once per month witches also celebrate an *esbat*, a Wiccan moon ritual when the goddess is honored. An esbat can be celebrated on a full moon or on any other phase of the moon. They are times for Wiccans to draw on their energy and do magick. According to Wiccans, each one of these celebrations happens at a time of heightened interaction between the supernatural and the natural worlds.[13]

Most Wiccans begin their year on October 31 with *Samhain* ("SOW-wen," or "sah-VEEN"). On this night they revere their friends and loved ones who have passed on to the other life. They also mark the symbolic death of the god on this night. This day is linked with the coming of winter. *Yule* is celebrated around December 21 (the date changes each year because of the solstices and equinoxes). On this day the rebirth of the god through the action of the goddess is celebrated.[14]

Wiccans celebrate the recovery of the goddess from giving birth to the god on *Imbolc* ("IM- bolk" or "EM-bowl"). It's a festival that takes place on February 1 or 2 for the renewing fertility of the earth. *Ostara* ("oh-STAR-ah")—the Spring equinox—is celebrated on or around March 21. It marks the first day of spring and the time of awakening of the goddess (earth) as the sun grows in warmth and power. April 30 is called *Beltane* ("BELL-tayne") and is the festival to recognize the young god venturing into manhood. He and the goddess—now his lover instead of his mother—fall in love and unite, producing the bounty of nature.

Midsummer, celebrated on or about June 21, is the time when the powers of nature (created by the union of the god and the goddess— sun and earth) are at their peak. This is a time when Wiccans gather to celebrate and practice magick. August 1 is known as *Lughnassadh* ("LOO-muss-uh"), which is the beginning of harvest. As the first fruits

---

[13]Sarah Hinlicky, "Witch Path Would You Choose?" *www.boundless.org,* 1999.

[14]A solstice is one of the two annual points on the ecliptic at which the sun's distance from the celestial equator is greatest; reached by the sun each year around June 22 and December 22. An equinox is one of the two times each year when the sun crosses the equator and, thus, day and night on earth are of equal length; happens around March 21 and September 23. The ecliptic is the great circle of the celestial sphere that is the apparent path of the sun among the other stars, or of the earth as seen from the sun.

and grains are cut, the god begins to weaken. The second harvest is called *Mabon* ("MAY-bon") and is celebrated on or around September 21. The god is preparing to die as the last fruits and grains are gathered.

This is a very simple description of the Sabbats outlining the completed cycle of rituals from Samhain to Mabon. The actual rituals can be much more intricate and elaborate honoring the god and goddess.

Wiccans believe in reincarnation, which deepens their need to "learn from all experiences." There's no actual heaven or hell, but instead they believe in a place called Summerland, where they believe their spirit goes after dying to think about the life it just lived, what it learned, and where it will come back next. Before each soul leaves Summerland, it will decide who it wants to be when it comes back and what lesson it will learn in the next lifetime. If a soul doesn't want to reincarnate right away, it can become a spirit guide. Ultimately, once a spirit has learned all it's supposed to learn and perfected this knowledge, it will be reunited and absorbed into the All.

Spell-casting and magick are a vital part of Wicca. Spells are seen as symbolic acts performed in an altered state of consciousness in order to cause a desired change. Spell-casting is a form of visualization also known as "guided imagery" or "mind over matter." *The Teen Spell Book*[15] says that spells and tools of the craft are only as powerful as the emotions they raise inside of you. For example, if someone believes that the color blue means "courage," then it will call forth that ability. Wiccans believe spells are primarily used to discipline the mind to create the fulfillment of their wishes. The book goes on to say that because they are so powerful, Wiccans must be very careful before they direct their intent or focus on anything.

Spell-casting also involves a number of ritual steps. A witch would start by casting a circle, then purifying and cleansing him or herself and any other participants. Following this they must ask for protection from the four directions and their guides, give an offering to the god and the goddess, and set up the cone of power.

A basic sacred text for many witches is something they call a Book of Shadows. It's called a Book of Shadows because magick works out-

---

[15]Jamie Wood, *The Teen Spell Book* (Berkeley: Celestial Arts, 2001).

side of time and space and in the "in-between" space of light and darkness, sounds and silences—the shadows. Plus, in the past witches would have to gather for their celebrations or exchange information in the shadows. A Book of Shadows is a spiritual diary that contains spells and spiritual thoughts, as well as formulas for the proper preparation of potions. This diary is where witches keep track of their feelings, experiences, and lessons they've learned. Anything and everything related to the craft experience can be put in one's Book of Shadows. It's like a personal reference book.

THE HISTORY OF WICCA

There's no real agreement as to the roots of Wicca. Some say Wicca is a direct religious descendant of the ancient Druids and Celts. Others claim it is much more modern—having been started within the last fifty or sixty years. Still other people believe it's at least twenty-five thousand years old. Starhawk, author of the book *Spiral Dance: A Rebirth of the Ancient Religion of the Goddess,* thinks that witchcraft had its beginnings close to thirty-five thousand years ago. No matter how old it really is, it's not until the third century that any substantial writing on witches and witchcraft can be found.

In 1401, at the instigation of Archbishop Thomas Arundel, the English Parliament established the first law specifically against witchcraft. An accused witch was given the chance to change her beliefs or be burned at the stake. In the years to follow, harsher penalties were attached to what would later be the Witchcraft Act.

In 1484 Pope Innocent VII wrote a letter about witches. This was not the first letter written by a pope on how to deal with witches, but it got more attention because, thanks to Guttenberg's invention of movable type, it was possible to print and widely distribute letters. The pope had written the letter because he was concerned that average people and clergy were not taking the threat posed by witches serious enough. Pope Innocent wanted everyone to help find the witches. The situation quickly got out of control as things like the *Witches Hammer*— a witch-hunter's manual—were printed, sparking panic and confusion resulting in the persecution of witches across Europe. Consequently many people were put to death. Today witches refer to this period of time as the Burning Times.

Witches and their beliefs survived the crucible—the severe trial of the Inquisition and the Middle Ages. Even though the persecution continued into the seventeenth century, it was much less widespread. In 1604 King James I—you might have seen his name on a translation of the Bible—passed the Witchcraft Act in England.

At the start of the sixteenth century, King Henry VIII provided the death penalty for witches who invoked or conjured an evil spirit; this led to witch hunts like those evident in the Salem trials. The Witchcraft Act of England was again used as law in Salem, Massachusetts, to prosecute people accused of practicing witchcraft. Maybe you've read Arthur Miller's play *The Crucible*, which tells the story of the Salem witch trials. The punishment for using witchcraft became hanging. After many years of witch trials, the act was finally repealed in 1736.

In 1736, under George II, a new Witchcraft Act marked a notable reversal in attitude. Now a person who pretended to have the power to call up spirits or foretell the future or cast spells was to be punished as a vagrant or con artist, and the penalty was a fine or imprisonment.

The last person to be convicted under the Witchcraft Act was Helen Duncan in 1944. Authorities feared that Duncan's alleged clairvoyant powers would enable her to betray (to enemies) details of the D-Day preparations. She spent nine months in prison.

From the eighteenth century onward, those who practiced witchcraft kept their knowledge and powers hidden and stayed out of sight. Because of this, a lot of people for decades thought witchcraft was dead, yet it was continuing to be passed down to succeeding generations. In the nineteenth century the intellectual community began to consider witchcraft in a different light. The English Parliament repealed the rest of the laws against witchcraft in 1951.

Wicca and Satanism may have the same root—denial of the truth—but after that point they really are very different. Wiccans today see their religion, with its origins in ancient occult religions like Druidism, as an acceptable worldview all by itself. Wiccans view Satanism as a distortion of the relatively "young" Christian religion.

Wicca is part of the neopagan movement—it attempts to revive the gods and goddesses and nature religions of ancient cultures. Wiccans and other neopagan groups draw from many sources including Gnosticism (salvation from this world being found through secret, mysterious knowledge), occult writings, Freemasonry (a widespread, secretive fraternal society), Native American religions, shamanism, spiritism, New Age philosophies, and even science fiction.[16]

The rise in modern witchcraft can be traced to people like Aleister Crowley, a renowned author of writings on magick and the occult, and Gerald Gardner, who came up with some new ideas so that the old image of diabolical witchery faded away and a whole new breed of witchcraft was born.

CONTEMPORARY WICCA

In the second half of the twentieth century, a revival of pre-Christian paganism occurred in the United States and Europe. The foundation of this revival was witchcraft, or Wicca (an early Anglo-Saxon word for witchcraft). The Englishman Gerald Gardner, who wrote the novel *High Magic's Aid* and the book *Witchcraft Today*, claimed that he was a witch initiated by a surviving coven, and imparted much of the alleged lore and rituals of English witches. This all came about after the archaeologist went to Southeast Asia and studied occult practices. He basically combined his Asian occult experiences with Western magical texts and developed a new religion with worship of a mother earth goddess as its focus.[17] Although his claims have been questioned, covens of modern witches sprang up under Gardner's inspiration and spread to the United States in the 1960s. This form of witchcraft consists of feelings for nature, colorful rituals, and a challenge of conventional religion and society.

In 1979 Starhawk wrote *Spiral Dance*, which has become essential reading for most witches. A whole new group of leaders began to emerge—people like Isaac Bonewits, with his practical guidance to liv-

[16]Alan W. Gomes, *Truth and Error: Comparison Charts on Cults and Christianity* (Grand Rapids: Zondervan Publishing House, 1998), 68.
[17]George A. Mather and Larry A. Nichols, *Dictionary of Cults, Sects, Religions and the Occult* (Grand Rapids: Zondervan Publishing Company, 1993), 314–315.

ing magick, and Scott Cunningham, sharing down-to-earth methods of witchcraft. Wiccan churches stopped popping up around the country, and online courses became available for those who wanted to learn more serious magick outside of a coven setting.

In 1986 a federal court ruled that Wicca is a legal religion and that the U.S. Constitution protects the practice of it. Some have estimated that in the United States alone there are between one hundred thousand and 1.5 million Wiccans, but the number could be a lot higher since Wicca is a self-styled religion.

Just like there are different denominations for Christians, there are various kinds of witches. Some witches practice rituals in covens, while others work alone and make up their own rituals. Still other witches follow a prescribed set of traditions.

The very nature of Wicca creates an atmosphere for all kinds of traditions to thrive. Here are some of the better-known traditions followed by witches today:

- **Gardnerian.** Founded by Gerald Gardner in Great Britain. It adheres to very structured practices, including ritual nudity and secretive initiations of new members.
- **Celtic.** Distinct feel of Druids with strong focus on the earth, the elements, and tree magick.
- **British Traditional.** Mix of Gardnerian and Celtic traditions. Structured in its practice and not very open to new members.
- **Kitchen Witch.** Focused on the practical side of earth and elemental magick and religion. Popular among city and suburban Wiccans, emphasizing magick in work and domestic environments.
- **Dianic.** Tagged the "feminist" movement of the craft. Mixtures of many traditions with a primary focus on the goddess, in particular Diana. Some have completely left out the male aspect of divinity.
- **Eclectic.** The most modern of the traditions that gives the freedom to mix and match whatever suits one best. Most popular form among Wiccans, especially those who practice it alone because it allows for complete freedom within the framework of the craft.
- **Faerie.** Based on faerie lore, combining natural magick with Celtic and Druid beliefs.

- **Pictish.** A Scottish tradition with very little religious content. Strong connection to nature and the animal, vegetable, and mineral kingdoms. A primary focus on magick.
- **Strega.** Dating back to 1353 in Italy, it is one of the oldest unchanged forms of witchcraft. They worship a god and goddess, meeter for full-moon rituals, and celebrate with singing, dancing, and sex. The celebration also consists of a feast of cakes and wine.
- **Teutonic/Nordic.** Rooted in the agricultural and warrior tribes of northern Germany and Scandinavia. The emphasis is on Nordic culture and the worship of the god Odin and the goddess Freya.

Music is also very important in Wicca, as it is in other religions. Music can be used in preparation for the ritual, or it can be used during the ritual. Magick meditation music or pagan dance music can be ordered online or bought at New Age or metaphysical stores. The group *Kiva* is a popular band that produces CDs of Wiccan dance music.

It all sounds pretty appealing—especially in a culture where there are no moral absolutes. After all, witches

- don't want to hurt anyone;
- believe in equal treatment of the sexes;
- accept any belief system because there is no one right way;
- want to live in harmony with nature;
- have access to a great depth of power;
- value sex as pleasure—they have no rules when it comes to homosexuality or pre-marital sex;
- don't worship Satan. Wiccans often say they don't believe in Satan or the devil and that he was just something Christians made up.

The big problem is that they're trying to live life completely independent of God. The craft is self-centered and encourages you to depend on yourself and the power within you. The God of Creation, who made you and me, says, "For apart from me you can do nothing" (John 15:5). Let's look some more at what God thinks about witchcraft.

WICCA AND CHRISTIANITY

Some involved with the craft believe that Christianity came from Wicca. Nothing could be further from the truth! All you have to do is compare the basic beliefs of each and you will see how different they really are. Since they both can't be right, ultimately it comes down to a choice to decide what you will believe and whom you will follow when it comes to spirituality and faith.

Both the Old and the New Testaments make repeated references to the practice of witchcraft and sorcery. In every instance where these practices are mentioned, God condemns them. The Bible condemns all forms of witchcraft, including sorcery, astrology, and magick.

Most Wiccans resent and reject the Bible. They view it as a Christian book with no experiential value and say it is completely out of touch with contemporary society. Yet there is more historical evidence to validate its truth than any other ancient writings. The Bible is God's "owner's manual" for our lives. For more details on why we can trust the Bible more than any other book ever written, check out chapter ten, "Whose Word You Gonna Trust?" I cannot find one book about Wicca that has any kind of support to give it the kind of authority that the Bible has.

God is so concerned about witchcraft and sorcery that He very specifically warns us in the Bible to stay away from it. In the book of 2 Chronicles we read the story about a man named Manasseh who became a king at the ripe old age of twelve. He did evil in the eyes of the Lord and paid a huge price for his bad choices. Here's what God said about Manasseh's involvement in witchcraft:

> Manasseh even sacrificed his own sons in the fire. . . . He practiced sorcery, divination, and witchcraft, and he consulted with mediums and psychics. He did much that was evil in the Lord's sight, arousing his anger. (2 Chronicles 33:6)

Just because this story is about a king who lived a few thousand years ago doesn't mean that God has changed His mind about witchcraft. This warning is just as relevant to us as it was in previous generations. Provoking God to anger is not a very smart thing to do. Why would God get angry about this kind of practice? Because He wants us to rely on Him for guidance, power, and direction. He is our strength and our life, not the forces of darkness.

God uses the Old Testament prophet Micah to warn the Israelites about going to witches for answers about life. "I will destroy your witchcraft and you will no longer cast spells" (Micah 5:12 NIV).

In the New Testament book of Galatians, the apostle Paul warns us to beware of the strong pull of our sinful nature that can cause us to rebel against God and sin.

> The acts of the sinful nature are obvious: sexual immorality, impurity and debauchery; idolatry and witchcraft; hatred, discord, jealousy, fits of rage, selfish ambition, dissensions, factions and envy; drunkenness, orgies, and the like. I warn you, as I did before, that those who live like this will not inherit the kingdom of God. (Galatians 5:19–21 NIV)

What an ugly list of sins witchcraft has been included in! Carefully consider Paul's warning at the end of this passage regarding the kingdom of God. The end of verse 21 is a reminder that if you continue to live in this kind of sin, you're in a dangerous position. It means your destination when you die will not be heaven. God uses even stronger language at the end of the New Testament.

> But cowards who turn away from me, and unbelievers, and the corrupt, and murderers, and the immoral, and those who practice witchcraft, and idol worshipers, and all liars—their doom is in the lake that burns with fire and sulfur. This is the second death. (Revelation 21:8)

We learn from studying the Bible that we get only one shot at life, and at the end God will hold us accountable for how we have lived.

> Each person dies only once and after that comes judgment. (Hebrews 9:27)

There is no opportunity to come back again and again to try to get it right. Heaven and hell are the ultimate realities for our eternal destiny.

Wicca also gives us some confusing information about the devil. The Bible confirms the reality of Satan and gives us an accurate picture of his true character.

In Ezekiel 28 (NIV) we learn much about Satan. Let's check out a few verses from this chapter in the Old Testament.

- "You were the model of perfection, full of wisdom and perfect in beauty" (v. 12).
- "You were blameless in your ways from the day you were created till wickedness was found in you" (v.15).
- "Your heart became proud on account of your beauty, and you corrupted your wisdom because of your splendor. So I threw you to the earth; I made a spectacle of you before kings" (v.17).

Satan was the wisest and most beautiful creature ever made, but he can only do what God allows him to do. Nothing else in all creation could compare to him, yet he made a horrible choice to rebel against God, ultimately plunging all of creation—including you and me—into a deadly spiritual war.

Satan's incredible pride led him to rise up against God. He refused to accept the fact that all of his greatness came from God. As his pride grew, he became determined to take over God's kingdom and seize control of His power. Satan, the most beautiful, the most powerful, and the wisest of all created beings, started a war he could never possibly win.

Because of His awesome holiness, God could not tolerate rebellion and evil in His kingdom. God stripped Satan of his position of authority, drove him from heaven, and made a disgrace of him as He threw him to earth. Though this battle between God and Satan started in heaven, we're now caught right in the middle of it here on this planet. And because Satan hates God, he also hates those of us who try to live our lives in a way that pleases the Lord. There's not a chance that the devil's going to let us remain untouched spiritually by his fierce attacks. He's going to throw everything he can in his arsenal of weapons to harass us and keep us from focusing on God, including trying to snare us with things like Wicca.

Wiccans say that Satan was just something Christians made up, but if you study the history of religion you'll find the concept of Satan in many ancient belief systems. Take Manichaeism for example. It was an ancient religion started by a Persian sage named Mani. Part of the doctrine of Manichaeism includes a dualistic division of the universe into opposing realms of good and evil. The light (spirit) was led by God, and the darkness (matter) was led by Satan. This same type of tradition can be found in other religions like Judaism and Islam.

But there's a distinction we need to make between other religious views of Satan and those of Christianity. In religions with dualism, the devil and God are equals; in Christian teaching they're not. The Bible teaches that Satan is a created being—a fallen angel—who is limited in his abilities and power, while God is all-powerful without any limitations apart from anything that contradicts His own perfection. And a big part of Satan's strategy in spiritual warfare is deception. Satan even disguises himself as an "angel of light" (2 Corinthians 11:14). Satan and his demons can deceive us by appearing to be attractive, moral, and good. Think about the appeal of Wicca and all the "good things it stands for."

The Bible is very clear that Satan not only exists, but he is also more than just an impersonal "force." You can say that you don't believe in him, but that doesn't change the reality of his existence.

God is not male and female; He is a Spirit pictured as our Father in the Bible. Because He is personal, there is warmth and understanding in our relationship with Him. He is not a department, a machine, or a computer that automatically supplies all our needs. He is an all-knowing, loving, good Father. He can be approached. God can be spoken to and He in turn speaks to us. Plus, our relationship with Him is not a one-way street. He doesn't just simply take and accept what we offer. He is a living and reciprocating being whom we meet and know.[18] In Isaiah 9:6 He is called Everlasting Father; Matthew 6:9 refers to Him as our Father in heaven; while in 2 Corinthians 6:18, God says He will be a Father to us.

The Bible also makes it clear that we are not to worship any other gods—including ones that we make ourselves.

---

[18]Millard J. Erickson, *Christian Theology*, 2nd ed. (Grand Rapids: Baker Books, 1998), 296.

"Do not worship any other god, for the Lord, whose name is Jealous, is a jealous God" (Exodus 34:14 NIV).

Why would God be jealous? One reason is because of His unconditional, sacrificial love for us. He demonstrated this love for us when He allowed Jesus to die for us on the cross (Romans 5:8). In all that I have read about the god and goddess of Wicca, there is absolutely nothing mentioned about them sacrificing or dying for anyone, to make a new and eternal life possible.

But let's look at this god and goddess issue from another angle. If we design and make our own gods (deities), they are actually smaller and less powerful than we are. So if we think logically, they are of no real value or help to us. We need a God that is bigger than us, one that we can turn to for guidance and power to deal with the difficult issues of life. How big is your God?

The Bible makes it very clear that Jesus is the only way to get to God and ultimately heaven. He is also the key to life on this planet (John 14:6). And did you notice that witches not only talk very little about life after death, but they also don't have a solution for the problem of sin and guilt?

Christianity and Wicca are mutually exclusive—at least one of them must be wrong. Compare the basic beliefs of each and see how different they really are. Ultimately you must make a choice to decide what you will believe and whom you will follow. Choose wisely, on solid evidence rather than on feelings and experiences that can change. There's too much at stake for this life and eternity not to give this all the attention it deserves.

CHAPTER THREE

WICCA GOES MAINSTREAM

I WAS SPEAKING AT A SUMMER CAMP in northern California and had just started working on this book. My friend Dave, program director at the camp, suggested I go into town and check out some of the bookstores for stuff on Wicca. Santa Cruz is a great beach town with lots of cool shops, things to see, and intriguing people to watch. My first stop was the Santa Cruz Bookstore. This place has books on just about any topic you can think of, including Wicca. I picked up a couple of books on the craft that I hadn't seen before and approached the counter to pay for them. The cashier was a twenty-something girl. I handed her the books and she asked me if I wanted "more stuff on Wicca." I answered, "Sure." She leaned across the counter and whispered, "If you want the real stuff, ya gotta go to Thirteen." "Aisle thirteen?" I asked. "No, go to Thirteen." "Section thirteen?" I questioned. "No," she said a little louder. "I'm not from around here," I said. She pointed to the front doors and said, "Go out those doors, cross the street. At the second block turn left. Go down the street and you'll see Thirteen on the right-hand side."

Now I felt like a counterespionage agent. I could hardly wait to see what "thirteen" was all about. A few minutes later I could see it—a small, plain-looking white storefront with a large numeral 13 hanging over the door. There was a guy and a girl sitting on a planter box out front dressed totally Goth from head to toe. I touched the doorknob and the guy jumped up, looked at me, and said to the girl, "Excuse me—I have to follow him."

I stepped in the door and he was so close to my back I could just about feel his breath on my neck. I quickly tried to take in all that was in the store. Over to my left was a woman sitting at a table reading tarot cards for a man. Straight ahead was a glass counter and some bookshelves all filled with a variety of items—everything from daggers to books to candles. To my right was a small room with floor-to-ceiling shelves, containing all kinds of herbs, powders, and potions. The guy shadowing me said, "Can I help you find something?" "No, I'm just looking right now," I said. He replied, "We have everything you need."

As I looked around, I couldn't believe my eyes. Everything I had been reading about and researching was right in front of my eyes. There were books of spells, clothing, and jewelry. I also saw wands, swords, pentacles, tarot cards, Ouija boards, and crystal balls. The store was incredibly well stocked with what seemed to be everything you'd need to practice the craft. I wondered just how many other stores there were like this in Santa Cruz and in other towns across North America.

HOW BIG IS WICCA?

Wicca is huge! It's everywhere—thanks to an extreme makeover that's happened in the media with witchcraft. Images of witches with pointy noses flying on broomsticks are gone. Instead, we've got Sabrina, Buffy, and the Halliwell sisters. Witches have been interviewed on the *Oprah Winfrey Show* and on cable news shows on Fox, CNN, and MSNBC. There's a whole new respect for witches today. If you're really trying to be politically correct, you don't talk bad about Wiccans. The Puyallup School District of twenty thousand students banned Halloween parties because they wanted to avoid offending the Wiccan religion.[1]

---

[1]MSNBC News, October 22, 2004, *MSNBC.msn.com*.

Every October witches and high priests and priestesses swoop down to the colonial town of Salem, Massachusetts. They come from all over the world, dressed in elaborate costumes, to attend the annual Halloween Witches' Ball. These wizards and mystics pay $150 to attend this gala, which is by invitation only. Hundreds attend and practice witchcraft, including channeling, tarot readings, and spells. The high priest of the Salem Witches, Shawn Poirier, produces the annual ball, where they conjure spirits of dead relatives, among other things.

According to the high priest, "It is a combination religious ceremony, rock concert, and New Year's Eve party." Poirier, who has been practicing Wicca for twenty years, also holds the only authentic séance in Salem, known as "Messages From the Spirit World." The town of Salem is notorious for the Salem Witch Trials of 1692, which pointed accusations at 150 townspeople and took nineteen lives by hanging on Gallows Hill. An Oscar-winning performance by Winona Ryder in Arthur Miller's *The Crucible* dramatically portrays the witchcraft hysteria started by two girls.

Feeling stifled by living in a community dedicated to serving God, the teenage girls dance naked in the woods. Abigail, who loses her virginity with a married farmer, drinks a charm to kill his wife. The girls are discovered and soon the entire village is consumed by cries of witchcraft. The local minister decides to rid the village of Satan and his emissaries—hoping it will reestablish his credentials as a man of God and save his job. A visiting spiritual expert in these matters decides to seize the moment for his fifteen minutes of fame and "uncovers" more of the devil's work that others who lacked his expertise had failed to detect. In the frenzy, one man denounces his neighbor so he can take over the poor man's property. A mom—disturbed and embittered by the death of her children—maliciously accuses other women of having favor with the devil because their children survived. Everyone who was not convicted and hanged profited from the witchcraft hysteria, including the Magistrate Danforth.

The popularity of witchcraft is evidenced among many college campuses also. Members of Syracuse University's Pagan Society lit candles in the campus chapel while curious students signed up for a new class on witchcraft. At the University of Arizona and Lehigh University in Pennsylvania, believers can be excused from class on Wiccan holidays. Anthony Paige, a recent SUNY Purchase College graduate who started a pagan student group there, said Wicca appeals to some college students because there is no sense of sin. Paige wrote a book called *Rocking the Goddess: Campus Wicca for the Student Practitioner*, which profiles college-age pagans.

Wicca is also making a fashion-trend statement. T-shirts with the word *Goddess* printed on them are available for both women and girls. There's the Earth Goddess collection of cosmetics. There are even "potions" fragrances showing up in some stores. All of these are just more messages that endorse Wicca.

As I write this chapter, there are well over one million Web listings for Wicca on Google. Internet resources on witchcraft are growing daily by the thousands. The Internet may be the source that has introduced more teens to Wicca than anything else. The world of witchcraft can be explored without ever leaving one's room. Wiccan teens can connect with others like them in a chat room or on a message board and discuss things that could end up in their Book of Shadows.

Through Wicca's huge online presence, one can take classes with the Academy of Sorcery, work on a degree or certification at Working Witches, or attend the Church and School of Wicca. There's even a Web site that will cast spells for you—100 percent satisfaction guaranteed. Luck, love, money, black magic. And there's tons of free stuff available for download or online ordering through thousands of other Web sites.

HARRY POTTER AND FRIENDS

Even though the Internet has become so huge in size and influence, it still will never replace books—in Wiccan culture or with the culture in general. According to the *New York Times*, Wicca is the fastest-growing, most lucrative subject in publishing today.[2] And Harry Potter is right at the top of the list.

---

[2]Fiona Horne, *Pop! Goes the Witch* (New York: The Disinformation Company, Ltd., 2004), 17.

British novelist J. K. Rowling has turned her childhood memories into literary magic.[3] Her Harry Potter book series is selling millions of copies and generating hundreds of millions of dollars in sales. The movies—based on the books—have a magic all their own. This bespectacled wizard, who attends Hogwarts School of Witchcraft and Wizardry, has exposed vast audiences to the world of witchcraft. With each book in the series, the story lines have gotten darker. But the line between fiction and reality has also been greatly blurred by Harry Potter. The Pagan Federation has appointed a youth officer to deal with the flood of inquirers following the success of the book series. Letters have been written addressed to Professor Dumbledore—Headmaster at Hogwarts—begging to be let into the school. It's like they want it to be true so badly, they've convinced themselves it's true. When I was in 13— the store in Santa Cruz—I saw many of the tools and potions mentioned in the Harry Potter books, but this was for real.

Carl McColman, author of *The Aspiring Mystic,* has put together a book called *The Well-Read Witch* to help anyone interested in finding the best books to read on Wicca. McColman reviews over four hundred books in his own paperback and also provides a basic overview of Wiccan spirituality. Llewellyn, one of the largest publishers of books on witchcraft, releases dozens of new books each year. *Teen Witch: Wicca for a New Generation,* by bestselling author Silver Ravenwolf, is one of the most popular books they have published, having sold more than any other book in their ninety-five-year history.[4] Llewellyn also publishes Scott Cunningham's book, *Wicca: A Guide for the Solitary Practitioner,* which is probably one of the most widely read books on Wicca and has sold over four hundred thousand copies. Llewellyn has developed quite a catalog of fiction and nonfiction witchcraft books for teens, consisting of titles like *Spellcraft for Teens: A Magickal Guide to Writing and Casting Spells*; the *Witchy Day Planner*; and *Teen Goddess: How to Look, Love, and Live Like a Goddess.*

There's also been a huge increase in the number of local publications. I recently picked up a copy of a quarterly pagan magazine

---

[3]Raffaella Barker, "Harry Potter's Mum" (*Good Housekeeping,* October 2000), 85.
[4]"Teens & Wicca—Why (and how many) youth are drawn to Wicca," *www.religioustolerance.org/wic_teen1.htm.*

called *The Community Seed*, which claims to be an organization supporting pagans and other earth-based spiritualists through community service, publications, events, and other ritual celebrations. *The Community
Seed* defines a pagan as "one who follows their own unique spiritual
path, honoring both male and female aspects of deity, and in tune with
their connection to the Earth, the Elements, and the turning of the
seasons."

All of these publications and more are giving Wicca "an extreme
makeover" and helping it to become more widely known.

MEDIA MONSTER

When the movie *The Craft* was first released, it triggered a huge
increase in the number of people contacting Wicca groups online. The
film, about a modern-day coven of young witches, is about three high
school outcasts who practice witchcraft but struggle to attain the kinds
of results they want; they need a fourth member of the coven. That
role is fulfilled by the new girl in town, Sarah Bailey. Sarah seems to be
a normal high school student, yet we soon learn that she has a history
of making things happen around her when she's upset, and that this
problem has led to one suicide attempt in the past. The three resident
weird girls at school soon recognize Sarah's inherent magickal abilities
and bring her into their circle. The leader of the group is Nancy
Downs, a tough, unstable girl who oozes attitude from every pore in
her body. She has a much deeper interest in the uses of magick than
her "sisters," Rochelle and Bonnie, and the fact that Sarah seems to
have more in the way of magickal potential than she does gnaws away
at her over time.

After first succeeding at a few parlor-trick types of magic, the girls
put their powers to more serious use. Bonnie asks for the scars she was
born with to be removed; Rochelle wants payback against a cruel, racist
girl at school; and Sarah wants the creep of a guy she likes to fall in
love with her. Nancy has larger ambitions, invoking the spirit of Manol
and all his powers. (Or "Manon"—the fictitious name given to this
spirit that supposedly represents the one beyond everything, or the All.)
The spells begin to work, but they work a little too well, leading to

some pretty significant internal troubles for the coven.

Charmed, another story about a coven of young female witches, has become a huge hit on the WB television network. The Halliwell sisters—Phoebe, Prue, and Piper—each have a big problem in life. Prue and Piper both have hard-to-please bosses, while Phoebe can't seem to keep a job. One day Phoebe starts playing with a Ouija board when it mysteriously spells out *attic.* Phoebe ventures up into the attic and finds a mysterious book labeled *The Book of Shadows* in a glowing chest. Phoebe reads a spell that releases the sisters' powers, and they discover that they're descendants of a line of female witches. Each one has a special ability—moving objects, stopping time, seeing the future—and they can also combine their abilities into the "Power of Three" to fight demons, warlocks, and other evil beings.

Do you remember *Sabrina, the Teenage Witch?* Sabrina Spellman thought she was a normal sixteen-year-old until her aunts—Hilda and Zelda—told her that she is a witch, along with her whole family on her father's side. While preparing to get her witch's license, Sabrina ends up living with her aunts in Massachusetts. Sabrina gets into several scrapes as she tries to figure out how certain spells work.

Then there's the *Bewitched* movie starring Nicole Kidman and Will Ferrell. Based on the classic TV show from 1964–1972, *Bewitched* is a romantic comedy about an entire family of witches who are immortal. One member of the family is a beautiful witch named Samantha who marries a mortal husband and promises to give up her special powers— much to the disapproval of her relatives. These witchy relatives are constantly interfering in the marriage by using their magic in mischievous ways. And Samantha herself struggles with the temptation to use her magical powers to get things done around the house.

How about Saturday morning television? Themes of witchcraft and sorcery can even be found in cartoons like *Sabrina, W.I.T.C.H., Scooby Doo,* and *Shaman King.*

No doubt the media have helped witchcraft gain a much bigger presence in society in the last few years. Wicca is everywhere!

WHAT'S THE DEAL WITH WICCA?

Wicca has gone from a scorned and ridiculed superstition to a mainstream religious system touted as the preferable alternative to "outmoded Christianity." To a lot of kids today, following Jesus doesn't seem relevant anymore; they can't seem to find the "spiritual experience" they're looking for when they go to church. Something's missing, and a number of teens are convinced they can find it in the craft.

More and more famous celebrities, authors, and entertainers have discovered the goddess. I mention a few of them in the chapter on "The Girl-Friendly Religion," but the list also includes people like Olympia Dukakis, Marianne Williamson, Deepak Chopra, Erica Jong, Camille Paglia, and Fairuza Balk.[5] Musician and songwriter Sting sought help from Michele Morgan, an author and tarot card consultant, for his CD-ROM *All This Time*. As celebrities have brought witchcraft to the attention of the media, the public has listened. Many would say it's now the fastest-growing spiritual practice in America.[6]

Wicca's popularity has been growing for a long time. Besides the push from the media, fashion trends, and celebrities, Wicca also got some help from the legal community. In 1986 a Federal Court of Appeals decision (*Dettmer v. Landon*) declared The Church of Wicca to be a constitutionally recognizable "religion," giving it the same legal rights and standing as other religions. This was one more thing that witches used to help change their popular image. But more than anything, the changes in our culture—especially with teens—helped Wicca escape the occult ghetto and go mainstream.

Two main things made this possible. One was the awareness among teens of something called "dark spirituality." As more and more teens were feeling alienated by society and their families, they turned to the "dark side." The emphasis was on power—pursuing it and using it by occult means that included divination, witchcraft, and sorcery. Fantasy role-playing games were a big part of this. Fast-forward and dark spirituality was mainly connected to the Goth movement. Gargoyles, vampires, gloom, depression, and nihilism seemed to characterize this "tribe" or teen subculture.

But something else has paved the way for Wicca: the lack of absolutes in our society. This isn't something that just all of a sudden happened, but relative truth is definitely here to stay. Less than ten percent

---

[5]Horne, 16.
[6]Ibid.

of teens believe there are moral absolutes. Kids were ready to respond to a "buffet-style" religion like Wicca.

So what's being spelled out in the Wiccan sales pitch that teens today are buying? There are a lot of things that kids find appealing, starting with power. The promise of power over one's circumstances is huge. Everything from cones of power to magick is at your disposal, according to Wicca. Witches believe spells can find someone to love you, make you glamorous, have a happy home, rid yourself of guilt and shame, keep cash flowing, take care of a crabby teacher, or get ungrounded.

Then there's the elevation and empowerment of girls and women or a sensitivity to and protection of the environment. There's the sense of belonging that comes with being initiated—whether it's into a coven or as a solitary practitioner of Wicca. And there's the knowledge of the magick circle, which functions as a church, holy ground, or place to hold one's power until they are ready to release it. One of the other big things is the opportunity to put together one's own set of beliefs and create one's own moral and ethical framework for life.

Wicca appears to offer everything a teenage guy or girl could want or need to make sense out of life. But can and does the craft really deliver the goods? Let's look at the elements of Wicca that are explored individually in the following chapters.

CHAPTER FOUR

THE ALLURE OF PERSONAL POWER

KAYTEE IS A LOT LIKE OTHER SIXTEEN-YEAR-OLDS.
She struggles at school and at home. She's fascinated by the supernatural, dreams of being an actress someday, and is searching for power to
make her dreams become reality. However, Kaytee is also a Wiccan. So
are her mother, her father, and her eight-year-old sister. Kaytee's parents
are first-degree witches, but she is still practicing for initiation.

Right now she's learning the basics of the cone of power and about
the gods and goddesses of the magick circle. Everyone at school knows
she's into witchcraft, although most don't understand it. Kaytee says she is
going to use her first spell to help her get the part of Peter Pan in the
school play. "It's like prayer," she says. "I will project that I will get this
part of Peter Pan in the musical, harm me none and for the good of all."

GRADES OF INITIATION

Let's spend a moment on Wiccan "degrees," mentioned in Kaytee's
story.

Wicca is often described as a non-hierarchical religion, which many people see as a system's spiritual strength. It calls for active individual participation (rather than passive observation) in group rituals, acknowledging each individual's responsibility for spiritual progress. Even so, Wicca has three degrees, or grades, of initiation, and a system of coven leadership that seems to bear many traits of an organizational-hierarchy model.

The first degree is for those newly coming into the craft. It consecrates them as a priest or priestess and witch, and they are trained in the techniques of the witches' magickal art. The new witch is initiated into the coven and participates in the religious rites and spiritual life of the group.

The second degree marks the beginning of a deeper path within the craft, acknowledging the commitment, work, and effort made by candidates following first-degree initiation. Witches are consecrated as high priests or priestesses; they also have attained sufficient proficiency in the craft so that they can share in the responsibility for the coven's religious and spiritual life.

The third degree is granted to those of sufficient experience and knowledge who are either in a working partnership together and are going to leave their parent coven to form a new one, or to individuals working without a craft partner who will become an elder of the craft and form a new coven of their own. The third-degree witch is not a "perfected individual" but a person in the process of achieving spiritual individuality for which the work of the first two degrees has laid the necessary foundations. Elevation to the third degree recognizes witches as having so sufficiently mastered the craft that they are able to take on the responsibility of guiding others on the path of independence, and with full authority as a Wiccan high priest(ess).

TOOLS OF POWER

Witchcraft. The very word stirs deep emotions, visions of mysterious rites done in dark of night, and thoughts of ancient occult secrets. Those secrets both lure and frighten you. They hold the promise of power— power to improve your life; to gain the serenity, love, and comfort you have always wanted; and to stop your enemies cold in their tracks.[1]

---

[1]Gavin & Yvonne Frost, The Magic Power of White Witchcraft (Paramus, NJ: Prentice Hall Press, 1999), 1.

Teens are turning to the craft today because this religion appears powerful, glamorous, and definitely not the norm. Those involved in Wicca claim to have a depth of power far greater than the average person seems to have. According to the Web site for the Church and School of Wicca, this previously underground religion has much to teach every human about survival and the ethical use of natural intrinsic powers.[2]

Supposedly the creative power of the universe lives in everyone. Those who practice Wicca believe in the "power within" rather than the patriarchal religions' belief in the "power over." They also believe in going with nature rather than against it. The key is for individuals to learn about the powers hidden within them that they have not developed, say Gavin and Yvonne Frost, founders of the Church and School of Wicca. Scientific experiments clearly show that people are linked together telepathically. People can use that telepathic link to help themselves, both by making other people do their will and by reading the innermost secrets of others. It is the practice of such control and development of people's ability to direct their powers that will equip them for their new life.[3]

Thoughts can turn into action. Wiccans think of things that they would like to change, and then transmit those thoughts with the aid of magick power. The thoughts will speed to their target and cause those desired things to become reality—gaining power over others as well as gaining material things.

Wiccans believe awesome resources are available to the initiated witches who have full knowledge of their powers. This knowledge includes not only learning how to build one's power, but also discovering the time of day that power is the strongest. In the process of developing personal magick power, witches need to remember a number of affirmations relating to their personal power. These phrases are meant to help validate, confirm, and state in a positive way what they're trying to achieve. Here are some examples:

- I am alive. I have power. It is real.
- My witchcraft power will achieve my goal.

[2] www.wicca.org.
[3] Frost, 2.

- I am grateful for all that has been given to me in the past.
- I am grateful for all that will come to me today.
- I will achieve victory through good health.
- By Aradia, I will win.
- I will give and receive true love.
- They are hidebound; I can adapt.
- My guide is here to help me.
- I can separate my spirit from my body.[4]

When used, these affirmations or phrases should be stated in a powerful, explosive way.

This power is drawn from several sources, including spirit (god, according to their definition), the elements, the ancestors, and the angels. Witches use their own power—power of the mind—to manifest what they need. They believe that over the centuries, humans have become lazy and suppressed many of their instinctive talents, including the power of the mind, and that we access only what we think we need and apparently don't bother to use a huge portion of our mind power. It's from this "unused mind" that abilities such as clairvoyance, telekinesis, and extrasensory perception (ESP) are found. According to those involved in Wicca, everyone has these abilities, but most people don't use them—sometimes because of fear. However, witches and other enlightened souls strive to strengthen these natural gifts.

Wiccan author Scott Cunningham reminds witches that although personal power is the most potent force at work in folk magick, its practitioners utilize a wide variety of magickal objects borrowed from the spells and rituals of various cultures. Such "tools" are used to lend their own energies, as well as produce the state of consciousness necessary for magickal workings. Folk magicians have always used natural objects as well as expertly crafted tools to strengthen their magickal rituals.[5]

---

[4]Aradia, a goddess frequently mentioned in Wiccan rituals, is from the Italian pantheon. She is known as the queen of witches—filled with power, she can be called upon to protect any witch.
[5]Scott Cunningham, *The Truth About Witchcraft Today* (St. Paul: Llewellyn Publications, 1987), 27.

THE CONE OF POWER

The cone of power is one of the sources of a Wiccan's power. The three-sided witch's hat, which looks like a triangle, is a symbol that represents the cone of power. According to Silver Ravenwolf in her book *Teen Witch*, witchcraft encompasses three sides (angles) of belief: love, positive creativity, and spirit. Love can soothe the soul, open a door, and make us all one. The witch does his or her best to love all creatures big or small. The bottom of the hat, or foundation of the craft, is love. The second side of the hat is positive creativity. Wiccan belief states that the main purpose of being human falls under the art of creation or how one invests their time. It doesn't really matter what people do as long as they create in a positive way. Spirit (or the lord and the lady) makes up the third side of the hat. Witches believe that god—in whatever form—exists, is within us and around us, and is willing to help us if we only ask. God is often called the lord and the lady, because witches see god as both masculine and feminine. Other times god is called spirit. Allah, Jesus, and Buddha are all said to be faces of the masculine side of god. Wiccans also give equal importance to the feminine side of god. By putting the three sides of the hat together—love, positive creativity, and spirit—Wiccans create a cone of power from which their magick energy or power comes from. Witches believe they can do and make miracles happen for themselves and others through the cone of power.[6]

CRYSTALS AND STONES

One of the more recent rediscoveries of ancient folk magick is the use of stones and crystals. Many books have been written about the magic of stones and their ability to improve people's lives. Witches not only appreciate crystals for their intrinsic value and beauty, but they also believe stones contain specific energies for magickal use. Some believe that along with herbs, stones may have been the first magickal tools of ancient times.

Clear and colored varieties of quartz crystals are used, including amethyst (purple), carnelian (orange), citrine (yellow), blue quartz, and

---

[6]Silver Ravenwolf, *Teen Witch* (St. Paul: Llewellyn Publications, 2000), 10.

rose quartz. Witches use many other types of stones besides quartz to gain better health, draw love, attract money, bring peace, and protect against a variety of illnesses. There are more than a hundred stones used in magick that Wiccans believe can be called upon to release or absorb power. Here's a sample list of the stones and perceived benefits:

Diamonds—strength, reconciliation, healing, and protection
Emeralds—love, money, health, and psychic powers
Sapphires—meditation, peace, and power
Rubies—joy, wealth, and restful sleep
Fluorite—mental acuity
Sugilite—psychism, spirituality, and healing power
Kunzite—peace and healing

Folk magicians claim to have the ability to work with these "tools" to arouse, program, release, and direct energies within stones. Once they are empowered, these stones are worn, carried, slipped under a mattress, or placed on magickal altars. In the case of crystals, they are stroked on the body and placed around the house to release their beneficial energies.

HERBS

Wiccans view herbs like crystals—possessing specific, distinct energies that can be used in magick. They collect, mix, burn, and brew these seemingly fragrant treasures. A wide variety of herbs—encompassing fruits, trees, flowers, roots, nuts, seeds, seaweeds, ferns, grasses, and all other types of plant materials—are used in folk magick.[7] Here's a sampling of herbs that are being used by modern witches and their perceived benefits:

Cinnamon—burned to stimulate intelligence
Rose petals—strewn around the house to promote peace; placed
    between pink candles to bring love into the witch's life
Lavender flowers—added to a bath for purification purposes
Sandalwood—burned to heighten meditation and psychic experiences

Witches believe that the power of herbs can be released in a couple

---

[7]Cunningham, 30.

of ways. They can be carried in a pocket, sprinkled around the house, or burned as incense, thus releasing their energies into the air. In the form of oil, they can be blended and rubbed onto the body or added to the bath, or they can be used to anoint crystals or other objects in rituals.

CANDLES, COLORS, AND CORDS

Wiccans use candles as magickal tools in two ways: as focal points for power and as additional magickal energy that comes from the colors and flames. In some rituals, depending on the magickal goal, candles of specific shapes and sizes are burned. However, most of the time the candle is a simple common shape, and it's the color that's of great importance to the magick ritual.

Psychologists have come to realize that colors can have strong effects on our bodies as well as our subconscious minds. For example, hospital rooms are often painted in soft shades of green or blue to stimulate healing. Prison walls are painted pink so as to calm down violent or disturbed prisoners. Red is used to attract attention as in advertising or with Stop signs and emergency lights. Wiccans also feel that colors have subconscious effects, and they believe candles contain certain energies related to color. When performing rituals, Wiccans carefully select colored candles based on the need. Here's a sample list:

Yellow—intelligence, divination
White—purification, protection, peace
Green—money, fertility, growth, employment
Light Green—improve the weather
Blue—healing, psychism, patience, happiness
Black—negation, absorption of disease and negativity
Red—protection, health, strength, courage, exorcism, passion
Purple—power, healing of severe disease, spirituality and meditation
Dark Purple—calling up the ancient ones
Brown—healing of animals, homes
Dark Brown—invoking earth for benefits
Orange—material gain, to seal a spell, attraction
Pink—love, friendship

In rituals, candles rubbed with fragrant oils are placed in special holders and surrounded by crystals. Various symbols are sometimes scratched on the candle's surface, while herbs are piled up around their bases or scattered on the working area. The witch then lights the candle and, as it flames, begins to visualize his or her need. The flame of the candle, as well as the objects around it, helps to direct the witch's personal power. A witch must be careful to snuff out the candle, not blow it out, otherwise the magick is blown away.

Wiccans use candles to serve as focal points of natural and personal power in magick rituals. However, one of the most powerful effects of candles is their ability to alter our conscious minds.

Magick with cords is one of the more simple operations that can be used, either alone or with other tools of power. Simple cord magick involves the following:

- choice of cord color
- choice of cord length
- choice of disposable cord, or one you will use again
- choice of divinity

Usually cord magick involves a black, white, or red cord (basic colors of early goddess worship), thirteen inches in length, with the plan of disposing of the cord when the ritual is done.

Cord magick requires the magickal operation of "charging," where each knot is charged with a chant or charm. Disposal depends on the purpose of the spell. Magick is released by drawing a star in the air over the cord while picturing the magick seeping away from the item.[8]

WORDS, CHANTS, AND POETRY

In relationships, words are the main way of communicating. Despite the highly technological times we live in, for many it's still the only understandable way of sharing thoughts, emotions, and experiences.

An important part of Wiccan magick is the breath as well as the sounds and words produced with it. For generations, secret chants and words of power have been passed down from one witch to another.

---

[8]Ravenwolf, 114.

Witches speak words to herbs, stones, and candles during magick rituals designed to program and stir up their energies. They also use magick words to communicate with the power that's inside them. Words alone are not thought to bring about change; rather, they're used to assist in pinpointing a witch's concentration and to allow him or her to perform a particular magickal action. Basically, when a witch speaks to an object (candle, stone, etc.) they're really speaking to their inner self.

Wiccans believe that poetry is one of the most potent forms of ritual speech. It touches the unconscious mind, the mind of dreams, psychism, sleep, and magic. Rhymed words are easier to recall and flow smoothly during rituals.[9] The words used are very important because of their ability to fill the witch with the proper state of mind, allowing him or her to move energy. The words must have personal meaning to the individual witch. Some witches prefer to compose a fresh, simple rhyme that speaks to them rather than use ancient words of power that may be meaningless to them. Words that speak to a witch can be adequate to produce the necessary state of mind and get the power moving.

TECHNIQUES AND OBJECTS

There are many other techniques and objects used by Wiccans in magick rituals. Here's a quick sample:

Knots—used to represent the physical manifestation of a spell. They are used to lend protection to a person or place.
Clay—molded into symbolic shapes.
Mirrors—used to reflect evil and awaken psychic awareness.
Ink—used to create shapes or draw runes.
Sand—poured into specific images (like sand painting).
Water—used for purification.
Food—prepared for specific magickal changes.
Runes—symbols containing within their lines specific energies.

There are lots of rituals and spells. Witches will often make use of two or more of the power tools that we've looked at in this chapter. Each element is used in a specific way to enable a witch to achieve the necessary results.

---

[9]Cunningham, 34.

DAYS OF POWER

Most religions have holy days throughout the calendar year. Wicca is no different. However, to witches these days aren't just holy, they're days of power. Most Wiccans perform rituals at least twenty-one times a year: thirteen full-moon celebrations—goddess-oriented—and eight solar festivals related to the god. These rites are done by individuals or in covens.

ESBATS

An esbat is commonly known as a Full Moon Ritual. It's a rite that involves the worship of the goddess and a magickal working. Wiccans often gather with their coven on nights with a full moon (every twenty-eight days) for a magickal ritual. They view the moon as a symbol of the goddess, and they also see it as a mystical source of energy because it reflects light from the hidden sun—light can be equated with power—and because the moon has proven strong effects on the tides and cycles of both women and animals. During esbats, Wiccans draw energy from the moon to gain more power in their magickal workings. Esbats are a time of reverence and magick as well as sanctity and spirituality.

SABBATS

While the moon determines esbats, Sabbats are decided by the changing of the seasons. They're connected with ancient European planting and harvesting rites; ancient hunting ceremonies plus the solstices and equinoxes. Just like esbats, Sabbat rituals are held at night. Sabbats basically tell the story of a Wiccan legend about the god and goddess. The details of this legend can be found by examining the eight Sabbats of the calendar year.

For many Wiccans the year begins on October 31 or *Samhain*. On this night they venerate their loved ones and friends who have died. Because Wiccans believe in reincarnation, this is more of a quiet celebration rather than a somber one. Samhain is also linked with the coming of winter and ancient hunting rituals. Plus, this is the night that Wiccans mark the symbolic death of the god.

December 21 or 22, or *Yule*, is the date of the solstice each year.

This day commemorates the rebirth of the god (symbolically seen as the sun) through the work of the goddess.

Imbolc (February 1 or 2) is the day when Wiccans celebrate the recovery of the goddess from giving birth to the god. It's a festival of reverence and purification for the renewing fertility of the earth.

March 21 is *Ostara* or the spring solstice. Wiccans see this as the time of the awakening of the earth (the goddess in her terrestrial side), as the sun grows in power and warmth.

April 30 is known as *Beltane*. At this celebration the young god embarks on to manhood. He and the goddess (now his lover as well as mother) join together and produce the gift of nature. Keep in mind that according to Wiccan thought, the goddess and god are twin halves of a whole. They are dual reflections of the power behind the universe that can never be truly separated.[10]

June 21 is *Midsummer,* or the point at which the powers of nature (as a result of the union of the sun and the earth) are at their peak. This is a time for Wiccans to celebrate and practice magick.

August 1 is *Lughnasadh,* the beginning of the harvest. As the first fruits and grains are harvested, the god begins to lose his strength. Wiccans view Lughnasadh as their equivalent of Thanksgiving.

Mabon, on September 21, is the second harvest. As the last fruits of the harvest are gathered to nourish the people of the earth, the god prepares to die and leave this life behind.

Following most Sabbats are the sacred meals, or "cakes and wine." Foods that are representative of each Sabbat are placed on the altar and eaten during the sacred meal. Symbolic crafts may also be linked to the meal. In some instances magick rituals can also take place at this time. But most Wiccans keep the Sabbats as a time for worship.

Esbats and Sabbats can be seen on three levels. First, they are times of religious worship for Wiccans to connect with the god and goddess. Second, Wiccans use these days of power for working their magick to help, heal, comfort, and protect their friends and loved ones. They receive help in this process from other deities. Third, these are also times of celebration. Once the worship and work has been completed, it's party time!

---

[10]Cunningham, 116.

WICCAN MAGICK

Wiccans tackle lots of issues—even big ones like world peace and protecting the environment. Wiccan magick is also used to create a magick circle or sphere of power. This is where rituals are performed and tools are purified and charged for use in magickal ceremonies.

One of the most common methods that Wiccan covens use to raise energy is simply called "the dance." Because they see the human body as a storehouse of life-energy, muscular contraction produces readily available power for use in magick. Specific movements are used to build up energy during rituals. Here's how the dance works:

Once the religious rites have concluded, the coven leader (high priestess, priest, etc.) discusses the goal of the magickal rite to be performed by the group. Then the desired outcome is visualized in each person's mind, and a symbol of this may then be placed on the altar or written on a scrap of paper to be burned. Now the magick can begin. The Wiccans join hands and move clockwise around the altar, maintaining visualization. It's important to note here that clockwise motion (deosil) is thought to generate energy with positive qualities, while counter-clockwise movement (widdershins) draws energy with negative qualities. This is called "the dance" simply because the coven circles the altar with linked hands, not because they are actually dancing to choreographed steps. The coven then moves faster and faster until it becomes a blur to anyone who watches. During this time the witches are steadily increasing their energy. At the appropriate time, when the coven's power has risen to its peak, the group leader signals the members to release their energy and, through visualization, send it toward the goal. After the dance, the magickal rite is over. At this point the witches who participated may feel temporarily exhausted because of the expenditure of power.[11]

Here is where the need to recharge the cosmic battery comes into play. One of the easiest ways to recharge is to have a good meal, very high in red meat content, with red wine. After about three hours the cosmic energy level will have increased. For vegetarian Wiccans, power comes from a tree. A witch would simply stand under a large tree,

---

[11]Ibid.

preferably one with smooth bark, in the star position, facing the tree from the western side. Recharging occurs as they stand there for about five minutes with their forehead against the trunk. Yet another recharging option is to buy or build a large pyramid and sit under it. Sitting still in meditation for fifteen minutes also recharges energy.

WITCHCRAFT (MAGICK) CIRCLE

Influencing major events requires more power than the living body can contain. This is the time when the witchcraft magick circle is used. Usually this circle is found in a magick witchcraft temple. The temple is a special room or an isolated location outdoors and has been prepared in special magickal ways that include both a physical and a psychic cleansing. On the floor of the room are painted two concentric magic circles, each about one-half-inch wide. The circle defines the ritual area, holds in personal power, and shuts out distracting energies—it creates an atmosphere for the rites. It is constructed with personal power and is usually nine feet in diameter—the number of the goddess—but any size will work.[12] The first circle is used for personal magickal work, while the second circle is used for cosmic work.

In the craft no one may enter a magick circle unless they are properly prepared. This means that a person has either dedicated themselves to spirit, been initiated into the craft by other witches, or is willing to set aside any differences or negativity to work with the witches. To be properly prepared means that before entering the magick circle (the Wiccan church) the mind, body, and spirit have been cleansed of all negativity.[13]

PATHS OF POWER

The bigger the job, the more important it is to choose the right combination of tools. There are lots of tools that witches make use of for raising energy. These ways of raising energy are called paths of power. Some of these include

---

[12]Scott Cunningham, *Wicca: A Guide for the Solitary Practioner* (St. Paul: Llewellyn Publications, 2003), 57.
[13]Ravenwolf, 29.

- meditation
- invocation
- whispering, singing, monotonous chanting, or sing-song chanting
- trance and astral projection
- herbals, oils, and incense
- movement or dancing
- drums or rattles
- ritual

In any given magickal working, a witch may use more than one path of power.

SPELLS

Here's a basic outline of the rules Wiccans follow for good spells.

1. Confirm what is desired.
2. Decide on the motivation.
3. Decide what magick witchcraft method will be used to achieve the goal.
4. Define an alternate target or how excess power will be used.

The primary thing that makes spells work is the emotion invested in them. The right emotion enables a witch to send out an effective pulse of power. In the end, the spells a witch designs him- or herself carry more power than any spell found in a book. Those spells and magickal operations that are created alledgedly will meld creative energy with the forces of the universe.[14]

SIGNS AND SYMBOLS

The Wiccan religion has sacred signs and symbols of power that represent spirit. Here's an example of a few of them. (The symbols can be found in Appendix D.)

The five-pointed star, point up, is known as the pentagram. The pentacle is also a five-pointed star, point up, with a circle around the star. The pentacle stands for earth, air, fire, water, and the spirit of the

---

[14]Ibid., 134.

human, encompassed by the never-ending love (the circle) of spirit. Witches often wear this symbol for protection and as an affirmation of their beliefs. Wearing the symbol where everyone can see it isn't necessary; Wiccans believe the symbol carries more power if it's hidden.[15]

In magick a pentagram can be drawn several ways, depending upon the energy needed and the desired goal. The invoking pentagram is generally drawn starting at the top of the star and the banishing pentagram the exact opposite. The invoking pentagram brings energy inward, while the banishing one pushes negative energies away.[16]

The sacred spiral represents the dance of divine energy within the world of the witch. Drawn clockwise, the sacred spiral brings things toward the witch; drawn counterclockwise, the sacred spiral pushes negative energies away. The spiral also signifies the ancient journey within, because those who do not know themselves can never seek to know what may be outside them.[17]

The equal-armed cross stands for many ideals—the four seasons, the four directions, the four archangels, the four winds, or the four quarters of the magick circle. Drawn from top to bottom and right to left with the right hand, the symbol represents healing energies. Drawn from top to bottom and left to right with the left hand signifies banishing energies. A witch also uses the equal-armed cross to seal a magickal working so that the negative energies cannot reverse the positive efforts of the magickal person.

GOD AND GODDESS

In witchcraft there are many references to the god and goddess. These are additional tools of power available to Wiccans. However, these deities are much different than what you might think. Wiccans are referring to the gods and goddesses that have been created during the course of history by human beings. Prayer and worship to these mascots contain earth-level power that is stored in their images. The

[15]Ibid., 31.

[16]*Banishing* is to rid oneself of something or someone—for instance, if a witch wants to rid herself of an enemy, she can stomp out that person's path through the woods, symbolically taking power over his very footsteps. Invoking is to call forth energy from one's angels, spirit guides, god, goddess, and other spiritual beings.

[17]Ibid., 32.

gods and goddesses are a major source of power—which is available for witches to supplement the power innate in their living body.[18]

Despite all these tools of power available, Wiccans still maintain that you already possess the ultimate set of tools needed for life-changing power: your body and your mind. While Wiccans use their power to get what they want—heal someone, influence the boss to give them a raise, get the love of their life, or get vengeance on a bully at school—the bottom line is that witches utilize their power to help themselves and improve the quality of their life.

Gavin and Yvonne Frost ask the question, "What's wrong with your life?" They go on to detail the right each person has to a new life.

> No one, least of all kindly Jesus or gentle Buddha, expects or wants you to live in abject misery. So what is wrong with your life today that needs fixing today? Name it; then fix it. Consider what spell will be useful, get the equipment you will need, and get out of that chair and do it. We reminded you earlier that the gods help those who help themselves. You must put something into motion. It takes only a small and simple push; but once it is in motion, the result will be unbelievable. Use the following affirmation: Witchcraft power, give me a new life.[19]

All this sounds a bit confusing, doesn't it? Wiccans are trying to find the right combination of tools of power and some form of divinity in order to achieve a desired goal or cope with the problems of life, but when you step back and look at the big picture, you realize that the power Wicca offers is very self-centered, self-reliant, and limited.

THE SOURCE OF ULTIMATE POWER

Stop and think logically for a moment. If we lack the power (in ourselves) to begin with—to change our lives, help us cope or whatever the specific need may be—it's pointless to think that we will somehow be able to conjure up some untapped energy reservoir deep inside us. A chant, magick circles, poetry, symbols drawn in the air or worn

[18]Frost, 230.
[19]Ibid., 227–228.

around the neck, or even colored candles aren't going to help. The problem is that Wiccans continually rely upon energizing themselves (or some other object) with the use of one or more tools of power. But let's go a step further. Wiccans also believe that somehow you can obtain power from rocks, trees, and herbs. Think about it: Why would you look to a rock or herb for energy when you have the power to toss them in the air or grind them up to put in your food?

In reality, the energy that we need for living must come from a source outside ourselves. This source of power must be bigger than us, and it must be an unlimited supply of power or it's of no lasting value. This kind of power can only be found in one place.

It's described in a Book and is available to anyone who wants it. This power is limitless and can overcome even the most seemingly insurmountable problems. The source of this power is the living God— the God of the Bible. You say, "Wait a minute, Steve. Been there, done that." Have you? Have you really taken the time to carefully examine what the Bible teaches, or are you relying on faulty second-hand infor-mation? This is too important a subject to just take someone else's opinion. You need to look at the evidence for yourself.

I won't take time here to review the support presented in another chapter as to how we can know that the Bible is true, accurate, and a supernatural Book. Instead, let's look at some characteristics of God, described in the Bible regarding His unlimited, everlasting power that's greater than we can ever begin to comprehend. It's the only power that can truly transform your life.

Let's start by looking at God himself. Keep in mind that we're not talking about the human-made god (god and goddess, lord and lady, etc.) or the hundreds of little gods of the Wiccan religion. Nor are we talking about a God who hates women, as Wiccans have falsely stated in their literature. We're also not talking about the "god" within us or the one who dies and is reborn at a certain time each year, as we have seen described in the Wiccan Sabbats.

God is all-powerful and His infinite power is demonstrated in many ways. He is the One who forms us in our mother's womb (Psalm 139:13–16) and created the heavens (Jeremiah 32:17). Nothing is too hard for Him and He does as He pleases (Psalm 115:3). In ancient times

God's power over nature was frequently demonstrated in miracles: everything from the plagues in Egypt (Exodus 7–11) to calming a bad storm (Mark 4:35–41) and walking on water (Matthew 14:22–33). God's power is also obvious in His control of the course of history. In Acts 17:26 we read, "From one man he created all the nations throughout the whole earth. He decided beforehand when they should rise and fall, and he determined their boundaries." God is the chief Being in the universe, is all-powerful, and is able to do anything that is consistent with His own nature.

One of the greatest demonstrations of God's power is in how a human life can be changed. Check this out. "Those who become Christians become new persons. . . . The old life is gone. A new life has begun!" (2 Corinthians 5:17). God makes us brand-new people on the inside. Our attitudes, thoughts, and desires change. Sometimes even our personalities are different after we surrender our lives to Jesus. This is all a result of God's unlimited power.

Still, by far the greatest display of God's power was the resurrection of Jesus Christ from the dead. The Bible speaks of this power in 2 Corinthians 13:4: "Although he died on the cross in weakness, he now lives by the mighty power of God. We, too, are weak, but we live in him and have God's power—the power we use in dealing with you." There is overwhelming historical evidence to prove that Jesus did conquer death. The resurrection is not just a religious myth. Only Christianity has a God who became a man, to die on a cross for all people, and was brought back to life again in power after three days. Dead people can't help you, but Jesus can because He's alive! This same power that brought Jesus back from the dead is available to help us deal with the daily issues of life and give us hope for the future.

This power is available 24/7 to those who become followers of Christ—who have a relationship with God. Once we put our faith and trust in Jesus, the Holy Spirit comes to live inside of us, to give us power (John 14:12). Keep in mind that this is the same Holy Spirit the Bible teaches gave life to all of creation (Genesis 1:2). Talk about power! God doesn't want us to rely on our own limited strength and abilities. Instead, we're supposed to rely on the power God gives us through the Holy Spirit (Acts 1:8). This power not only helps us face the challenges of life but also enables us to make a difference in our world.

Stop. Before you go any further, I want you to think about something right now. Why would you want to worship and depend on a created object for power when you can go directly to the all-powerful Creator for help? Read the following verse from the Bible and carefully think about what's being said about you and the search for power.

> Christ is the one through whom God created everything in heaven and earth. He made the things we can see and the things we can't see—kings, kingdoms, rulers, and authorities. Everything has been created through him and for him. (Colossians 1:16)

Now think about the Wiccan tools of power that we looked at earlier. There were stones, crystals, herbs, colors, cones, cords, special days, molded clay symbols, little figurines, etc. Does it really make sense to depend on these objects for power when you can get power from the One who made them? The Bible actually talks about people like this who choose to follow a lie rather than the truth.

> They exchanged the truth of God for a lie, and worshiped and served created things rather than the Creator—who is forever praised. (Romans 1:25 NIV)

> All who worship idols will stand before the LORD in shame, along with all these craftsmen—mere humans—who claim they can make a god. Together they will stand in terror and shame. (Isaiah 44:11)

> There stands their god like a helpless scarecrow in a garden! It cannot speak, and it needs to be carried because it cannot walk. Do not be afraid of such gods, for they can neither harm you nor do you any good. (Jeremiah 10:5)

> Compared to him, all people are foolish and have no knowledge at all! They make idols, but the idols will disgrace their makers, for they are frauds. They have no life or power in them. (Jeremiah 10:14)

> Can people make their own god? The gods they make are not real gods at all! (Jeremiah 16:20)

> As you have seen and heard, this man Paul has persuaded many people that handmade gods aren't gods at all. (Acts 19:26)

Sometimes we're tempted to believe lies that reinforce our own selfish personal beliefs. Because Wicca is a religion of personal preferences, it's easy to see how someone could exchange the truth of God for a lie. Today, more than ever, we need to be careful about who and what we base our beliefs on.

The power that Wicca offers is limited and bogus. We're being deceived; it's spiritual warfare. Part of the devil's plan is to deceive us and counterfeit all that God is and does. He loves to disguise himself as an angel of light (2 Corinthians 11:14). Because he's a created being (Ezekiel 28:13, 15), his power is limited—in scope and ability.

Don't underestimate Satan and his demonic army. They can seduce us by appearing to be good, attractive, and even moral. He hooks us, deceives us, and sets out to destroy us. These evil spirits are not fantasies—they're real. We are up against a powerful enemy whose goal is to steal, kill, and destroy (John 10:10). Even though we can be sure of victory in the end, and our enemy is mortally wounded (Colossians 2:15), we are engaged in battle until Jesus takes us to heaven. Don't let your guard down—this is serious warfare! "Be careful! Watch out for attacks from the Devil, your great enemy. He prowls around like a roaring lion, looking for some victim to devour" (1 Peter 5:8). Don't be a casualty—remember who your commanding officer is!

Many unsuspecting people are getting sucked into the deception of Wicca. Don't be fooled by outside appearances. Ask yourself, "Does what they're teaching line up with the Bible? Do they confirm that Jesus is the only way to God?"

Don't be fooled because getting hold of power through the living God seems so simple—especially compared to what's necessary in Wicca to gain power. And don't get caught up in being able to explain and understand the capacity of God's supernatural power. There's an element of mystery to it; after all, God's power is supernatural. The greatest mistake we could make is to think that we could fully understand it. Daniel Webster, the great statesman and orator, was having dinner one evening with a group of scholars in Boston. The conversation around the table turned to Christianity. Webster clearly stated his belief in Jesus—the Son of God—and his dependence on Christ's death on the cross for the forgiveness of his sins. One man asked, "Mr. Webster, can you really comprehend how Jesus can be both God and man?" Webster replied, "No, sir, I cannot. If I could understand it—he would be no greater than myself. I believe I need a super-human Savior!"

How big is your God? Is he bigger than a crystal, an herb, or a cone of power?

It takes faith to believe in the God of the Bible. But it takes even more faith to try to make sense out of Wicca's source for power. If you really want the kind of power that can change your life and help you face the pressures of living in the twenty-first century, why would you want to rely on a created god who dies each year; on hugging a tree to get recharged; or on trying to get power out of a rock? The wise thing to do would be to find the source of unlimited power and plug into it.

When you decide to follow Jesus and establish a personal relationship with Him, you plug into all the power of the universe. The search for power begins and ends with Jesus. Rely on Him to give you the strength to overcome any struggle you may be facing today. Let this promise found in Philippians 4:13 encourage and guide you: "For I can do everything with the help of Christ who gives me the strength I need." It comes down to a control issue. If we really want God's power in our life, we have to surrender control and trust Him. That's not easy, especially in our self-centered world. And that's a big part of the appeal of Wicca—you're in charge, you maintain control. Yet when you realize how powerless you really are, it makes perfect sense to surrender to the living God and rely on Him to give you the power you need. Stop being deceived. Plug into the real source for power.

CHAPTER FIVE

THE GIRL-FRIENDLY RELIGION

THE WICKED OLD WITCH IS DEAD. That's not only a line from the classic movie *The Wizard of Oz*, it's reality in the world of contemporary Wicca. The old crone riding a broomstick wearing a pointed black hat with a wart on her nose and a black cat nearby has given way to a new breed of witch. Today's witch is young, is beautiful, practices magic, and wields mysterious psychic powers. One such example is the WB's *Buffy the Vampire Slayer*.

Buffy's TV show may be off the prime-time schedule, but the influence of this pop culture female witch icon is still being felt. Huge numbers of devout fans still watch reruns on TV or old episodes on DVD and video. Then there are the fans who read and collect the comics or the book series. Buffy is the classic female witch.

When the media pays attention to the Buffy character, they are generally not referring to actress Sarah Michelle Gellar, who plays her, but rather the fictional character Buffy Summers, who has entered the consciousness of thousands of fans—many who have never even seen the show. According to some Wiccans, this kind of attention that pop goddess-icons like Buffy receive is really energy, and an accomplished witch can use this energy in his or her works.

In her book *Pop! Goes the Witch,* actor, musician, author, and witch Fiona Horne talks about accessing the energy being directed to the Buffy character by all the attention. According to Horne, the key to accessing this energy from a target god or goddess is observation and getting an idea of their attributes. Then after careful observation and reviewing notes, one must weigh the pros and cons of making her into a god-form.[1]

Horne goes on to say that she came up with a list of attributes that she felt her Buffy god-form should have. After all, this god-form was her perception of Buffy, custom-tailored so that her energy could help her. Horne considered Buffy to be compassionate, empathetic, tough, strong, independent, determined, protective, and subversive to mainstream ideas.[2]

One night after creating an altar to Buffy (using fantasy books, a videotape, and a collage of images), Horne performed a ritual in which she created a link with the character. Horne "gave of herself" to the character and in return asked that Buffy act as her guardian when called upon.[3] Later in this chapter we'll look at the consequences of this kind of thinking.

Pop culture is filled with signs of the huge return of goddess-centered art, books, and music. Playwright Ntozake Shange said, "I found god in myself and I loved her fiercely."[4] Some witches would say it's because society is fed up with women being treated like second-class citizens in a male-dominated club. They're usually quick to point to Christianity as the main culprit because it has "taught" that women should be dominated. Wiccans believe that yang energy has been strongly emphasized through centuries of patriarchal influence and technological advancement.[5] Wiccans would say that the human spirit

[1]Fiona Horne, *Pop! Goes the Witch* (New York: The Disinformation Company, Ltd., 2004), 185.
[2]Ibid.
[3]Ibid.
[4]Marci McDonald, "Is God a Woman?" *Maclean's,* April 8, 1996, 46.
[5]Wiccans believe the sun and the moon symbolize the concept of the Chinese yin and yang. These are two opposing forces active in the universe. Yin exists in yang, and yang in yin. It's the changing combination of negative and positive, dark and light, cold and hot, which keeps the world spinning and creates Chi—the giving life-force. In all aspects of life, a state of balance should exist between the opposing forces of yin and yang.

now thirsts for a new and better balance with the goddess figure, so it's time to reclaim women's spirituality. Women across the continent are searching for new language and rites to reflect the feminine face of god.[6] Many celebrities like Fiona Horne have discovered and embraced this fast-growing spiritual practice in North America. The list of women who practice Wicca includes Tori Amos, Stevie Nicks, Sarah Mc-Lachlan, Cybill Shepherd, Roseanne, and Chrissie Hynde.

Witchcraft's public image continues to improve rapidly with teen girls. *Spin* magazine in its "Grrrl Power" issue ranked witchcraft as the top interest among teenage girls.[7] Ad campaigns targeting teen girls have featured actresses as witches, promoting many products including Finesse shampoo and Cover Girl cosmetics. And the appeal to females extended beyond teenagers when *YM Young & Modern* magazine featured two pages on witchcraft with the headline "Witchy Ways!" while *Jane* magazine featured Phyllis Curott, a high-profile witch, as one of their "Gutsiest Women of the Year."[8] Have you seen the bumper sticker "Back off: I'm a goddess" or the button that says, "My Goddess gave birth to your God"?

The Wiccan belief system can be a powerful invitation to teenage girls who feel held back because of gender or who have been victimized sexually or socially by teen guys or older men. Let's face it, being a teen girl today isn't easy, and Wicca can appear to offer you everything needed to not only survive but also live a satisfying and meaningful life.

FEMININE DIVINITIES

I receive lots of e-mails each month from teens on a variety of subjects, but questions and comments about Wicca happen to be one of the most frequent topics. Many of them talk about the god and the goddess (lord and lady) and the All. While I was writing this chapter, I received an e-mail from a girl who wrote: "I believe in a goddess that embodies the earth and is to me, as my mother." What's the deal with all this girl-friendly stuff?

---

[6]Ibid., 48.
[7]Brooks Alexander, *Witchcraft Goes Mainstream* (Eugene, Oregon: Harvest House, 2004), 49.
[8]Catherine Edwards, "Wicca Casts a Spell on Teenage Girls," *Insight*, October 25, 1999, 25.

The feminist movement in the late 1960s had a great deal to do with the resurrection of the craft and goddess religions. According to Michele Morgan—psychic, tarot counselor, and Wiccan—the craft has brought a much-needed counterbalance to the patriarchal systems that have dominated Western culture for years.[9]

According to Wiccan beliefs, way back in the beginning of time—before the earth and anything else—there was the All. The All, a female spirit, was all alone and existed in stillness and silence. She then created her other half—the male spirit. They entwined as one—the two halves of the whole—even though there are two spirits. Together they gave birth to the universe—solar systems, stars, moons, and planets. They also made land and water, plants, animals, and people on the earth.

Wiccans are more into the goddess because she represents the part of the All that is nurturing and compassionate, enabling growth, fertility, and gentleness. They also work with the goddess because of the nurturing fulfillment of her spirituality.

Wiccans believe that the goddess is in everything and is everything. She is not some force that looks down on us from above, but instead dwells in every single thing—in every rock, in every cat, in every drop of rain, and inside you.[10] This is also a key principle found in the New Age movement and is called pantheism. This belief allows Wiccans to worship the creation, mother earth (rocks, sun, moon, etc.), rather than the Creator (God).

As the feminine energies of the universe were being rediscovered, witches began looking at a variety of global goddess figures to find out what there was in common. The first place where there was unity was the maiden goddess. She is thought to be youthful, pure, optimistic, attractive, happy, brave, flexible, and full of enthusiasm. Usually the goddesses in the maiden group have celestial connections. Other symbols associated with the maiden include

- baby animals (before puberty);
- children's toys;
- colors of white and silver (for purity);

[9]Michele Morgan, *Simple Wicca* (Berkeley: Conari Press, 2000), 8.
[10]Denise Zimmerman and Katherine A. Gleason, *The Complete Idiot's Guide to Wicca and Witchcraft* (Indianapolis, IN: Alpha Books, 2000), 44.

- early hours in the day before noon;
- the season of spring to early summer;
- a clear piece of quartz;
- plants like the thistle, narcissus, chaste tree, and meadowsweet.

Also found in this category of maiden are goddesses of the dawn and spring as well as virginal goddesses.

Then there's the mother goddess. Her attributes include nurturing, maturity, and fruitfulness. This category includes goddesses of fertility, sexuality, and marriage. Some of the symbols associated with the mother include:

- dark, rich colors of red, forest green, and royal blue;
- geodes;[11]
- no-nonsense, functional clothing;
- the hours of noon to sunset;
- pregnant imagery like nursing animals, trees budding, and the pregnant goddess;
- the season of summer to mid-fall;
- plants like pansy, pomegranate, parsley, cowslip, and cinquefoil.

Finally comes the crone. Most of the time the images of the ancient crone are not very appealing. Usually you see her images at Halloween and the Celtic New Year—a festival to honor the dead. Her attributes include shrewdness, steadiness, enrichment, and cynical wisdom toward life. This category includes goddesses of fate, prudence, and ones who control the underworld, prophecy, and transformation. Symbols related with the crone include:

- robes and heavier clothing;
- dark colors of brown, midnight blue, and black;
- smoky quartz and fossils;
- the hours of sunset to dawn;
- plants like nightshade, mandrake, and holly;
- withered or dry items;
- the season of mid-fall to early spring.

---

[11] A sphere-shaped rock that contains a hollow cavity lined with crystals.

Much of Wicca is based on feelings and experiences, so when a witch feels like she or he needs more goddess attributes, there are several things that can be done. One possibility is to warm up some clothing in a dryer of goddess-centered herbs like gardenia blossoms, heather, lemon balm, lemon rind, lily, myrrh, primrose, spearmint, vanilla bean, and violet. By doing this the clothing will be charged with the goddesses' feminine attributes.

Another way to gain goddess attributes is to pick out an herb that's sacred to a specific patroness and use it in perfume or incense in honor of that goddess. Another option linked with this one is anointing candles and light bulbs. Finally, a witch may eat goddess-centered foods like coconut to internalize the lunar goddess, and he or she may wear clothing of a certain color to tap into a particular energy of the universe.[12]

Overall, the goddess energy is supposed to make witches more aware of their intuitive, spiritual nature. She's a reminder to be creative with magick and she gently motivates personal change. Novelist Susan Swan signed on for a unique spiritual tour—a pilgrimage to an ancient goddess shrine. Swan found herself struck by how powerful the female images of god were. "I do pray to a goddess-like presence. But I don't know whether she's a metaphor for my inner self or whether there's some spiritual force beyond the individual person."[13]

At first glance this sounds fascinating, intriguing—maybe even "warm and fuzzy." But let's step back for another look. In case you haven't noticed, this whole approach is very individualistic—nearly complete freedom of choice at the expense of any meaningful accountability. Besides some confusion, we're dealing a lot with feelings and experiences. There's too much at stake in life—on this planet and for eternity—to not carefully examine the spiritual dimension from more than one perspective.

JESUS, THE BIBLE, AND WOMEN

There are a lot of misconceptions about God's view of women. And there have been in the past and continue to be a lot of abuses of

---

[12]Marian Singer, *The Everything Wicca and Witchcraft Book* (Avon, Massachusetts: Adams Media Corporation, 2002), 247–248.
[13]Marci McDonald, "Is God a Woman?" *Maclean's*, April 8, 1996, 49.

women in the church today by men. Let's try to clear up some of this confusion by going right to the original source—the Bible—and starting at the beginning of human history.

The Old Testament book of Genesis says, "So God created people in his own image; God patterned them after himself; male and female he created them" (1:27). Both man and woman were made in God's image. Women have equality with men in creation. They are both at the very high point of creation and neither sex is higher or devalued.

In God's design women and men have different roles, but both have the same goals. God shapes and equips women and men for diverse tasks, but they all lead to the same ultimate goal—honoring Him. Each role carries exclusive responsibilities and privileges—and there's no room for the belief that one sex is superior to the other.

God has used women in awesome ways throughout history. He chose Deborah to lead the nation of Israel (Judges 4:4); Jael's resourcefulness and brave act rescued a nation (Judges 4:18–21); a woman's wise words and plan of action saved a city (2 Samuel 20:16).

Women had important roles in the early church. Check out what Paul writes in Romans 16:1–2 (NIV). "I commend to you our sister Phoebe, a servant of the church in Cenchrea. I ask you to receive her in the Lord in a way worthy of the saints and to give her any help she may need from you, for she has been a great help to many people, including me." Phoebe was a helper and highly regarded in the church.

Paul also made clear that men and women are spiritually equal: "There is no longer Jew or Gentile, slave or free, male or female. For you are all Christians—you are one in Christ Jesus" (Galatians 3:28).

There are amazing stories of women who held various leadership positions and were obviously the best people for the job because God chose them. Don't ever forget that God can use anyone to lead His people—male or female, young or old. Don't let the political correctness of our society or prejudices get in the way of leading or following someone. And be very careful of believing spiritual lies and deception that someone is trying to teach you.

Some people have been bothered because there were not any women among the twelve disciples, but it's clear that there were many women among Jesus' followers. Let's look at one example of the attitude that Jesus had toward women. It's in Luke 8:2–3. "Along with some women he had healed and from whom he had cast out evil spirits. Among them were Mary Magdalene, from whom he had cast out seven demons; Joanna, the wife of Chuza, Herod's business manager; Susanna; and many others who were contributing from their own resources to support Jesus and his disciples." Jesus raised women up from humiliation and servitude to the joy of partnership. Jewish culture forbade women to learn from rabbis, but Jesus treated women with dignity and respect. By allowing these women to travel with Him, Jesus was showing that everyone—men and women—is equal in God's sight.

Mary Magdalene was an early follower of Jesus who could have easily been called a disciple. This compassionate and energetic woman not only traveled with Jesus but also contributed to the needs of the group. Not only was she there when Jesus was crucified, she was also the first one to see Him after the resurrection (Mark 16:9).

This is quite a different picture about women than the ones painted by Wiccans or those at the forefront of the women's liberation movement. Don't let Wicca enslave you or a friend in a deceptive spiritual realm. Like it or not, if you're into Wicca, you're being deceived by Satan—who is your enemy. You may say that you don't recognize him, let alone consciously worship him, but that doesn't change the fact that you have bought his lie. For more on this, check out the section of this book where we discuss Wicca and Satan.

Think about what you're being taught and carefully weigh the evidence. If you search for the truth, you'll find it.

DO YOU KNOW YOUR FATHER?

I met Greg at a summer camp where I was speaking. Walking out of the dining hall after lunch, this football player yelled, "Hey, Russo—can we talk? Ya know that stuff about not knowing who your dad is that you talked about—that's me." Greg started to cry and said, "My dad divorced my mom when he found out she was pregnant. I've never seen or heard from him. It really hurts."

I've lost track of how many teenagers I have spoken with—in person or on talk radio—who've told me a similar story. Then there are the ones who tell me about an abusive father or one who is in jail. The bottom line is that there are a lot of people who either don't have a father or don't have a good relationship with him. So when you try to talk to them about trusting their Father in heaven, their response is, "Forget it."

The lack of a positive father figure in your life can make the goddess worship more appealing, and it can greatly affect your ability to experience the love and guidance of your Father in heaven. I think this is the case for many involved in Wicca. The pain associated with their earthly father has kept them from exploring a relationship with their Father in heaven.

What kind of relationship do you have with your father? I was very fortunate with my dad; he was a great father and friend. And even though he is now in heaven, the memories I have are of a man who loved and cared for me. Because I had such a good human father, I didn't have any obstacles to overcome when it came to establishing a relationship with my heavenly Father. But this may not be true for you. So let's take a look at what the Bible says our heavenly Father is like. But first, try to set aside the mental and emotional baggage you may have with your earthly father. I know it may be difficult, but it'll be worth it. Let's start by reviewing the story of the "Lost Son"—some Bible translations call him the Prodigal Son—in Luke 15:11–24. It's the story of a rebellious, immature young son who left home because he wanted to be free to live life as he pleased.

In this story we see the father watching and waiting for his son to return. He was dealing with a human being with a will of his own. The father in this story was ready to welcome his lost son back home, if he returned. This is a great picture of God, our Father in heaven. His love is constant and patient. God will give us every opportunity to respond, but He won't force us to come to Him. Just like the father in this story, God waits patiently and lovingly for us to come to our senses. Are you a lost son or daughter that needs to come to your senses? Come back to the One who loves you more than you could ever imagine. Let Him set you free to be the person you were created to be. And remember, God has all the power in the universe, and it's available to help put your broken heart and life back together.

But if you're still not convinced, check out these other places in the Bible that talk about your Father in heaven and what He's like. Take time to carefully read these verses and think about what they say. It's powerful stuff.

- Deuteronomy 32:6 talks about the "Father who created you."
- Isaiah 9:6 calls him an "Everlasting Father."
- First John 3:1 talks about how much our "Father loves us, for he allows us to be called his children."

This is not an exhaustive list of the characteristics of our heavenly Father, but it's a great place to start.

And by the way, if you're a guy reading this chapter, use Jesus as an example of how you should be treating women. Don't take your cues from our sex-crazed culture, where women are often pictured as something to be conquered to satisfy some out-of-control passionate need. Treat them as equals, with respect and dignity.

Don't allow yourself to be put down or demeaned. Remember that you're a unique creation of God with gifts, talents, and abilities others do not possess. Let your Father in heaven set you free and give you access to unlimited power only He can give to help you become the person you were created to be. Assume your role and responsibility as a young woman or man of God. Then watch Him work through you to change your world.

CHAPTER SIX

SIDING WITH THE ENVIRONMENT

SAMANTHA PRACTICES WICCA AND TRIES to protect the environment the best she can. "I know the god and goddess, or the All. I do think respect and care for nature are very important, but you must remember, as humans we are part of nature."

Wiccans view the earth as a living goddess, who blesses us and must be nurtured and cared for in return. They honor and work with the cycles of nature and the seasons rather than trying to dominate their environment. The Wheel of the Year—the Wiccan sacred calendar—is marked by eight festivals that celebrate the eternal cycle of life, as witnessed in nature by the changing of the seasons and the natural cycles of birth, maturation, death, and resurrection.[1] Ecological issues are of great importance to Wiccans, and consequently they've developed a reputation for being sensitive to and wanting to protect the environment.

Many Wiccans have become serious environmentalists in trying to "cause the least harm." The central principle in Wicca is the Rede, and

---

[1] Michele Morgan, *Simple Wicca* (Berkeley: Conari Press, 2000), 8.

in its somewhat archaic language it says, "An ye harm none, do what ye will." So the question most Wiccans ask a lot—especially when doing magick—is "How can I do the least harm?" They believe that "we are all one"—with spirit, with people, with plants, with animals, and with the elements.[2] Wiccans believe strongly in the integrity and freedom of the animal kingdom. Some witches are vegetarians, but those who do eat meat give thanks to the animal that gave its life in order for others to eat.[3]

Wiccans recycle trash, and some compost their food scraps or give them to animals to eat. Others buy only organic produce—vegetables and fruit grown in such a way as to cause the least harm to the earth and its inhabitants. If a witch cuts a branch from a tree, the next action is to give something back to the tree—some compost or leaf mold to help nourish its continued growth. When a witch harvests a plant, he or she tries to do it in such a way that is least harmful to the plant. Because Wicca is a nature religion, Wiccans see the goddess in everything. They not only see the goddess in everything, but Wiccans honor the goddess in everything by living in harmony with nature.[4]

Wicca allows one to develop a constant, interactive relationship with spirit in as simple a way as seeing the moon come up through the trees and feeling a breathless kinship to her beauty and power, to receiving specific assistance for anything from finding a parking space to mending a relationship.[5] Wiccans believe that we (humans) have an undividable relationship with the earth.

A lot of these ideas sound pretty good and responsible. I think most people would agree that we all need to do more and work harder to protect the environment. A century ago, concern over exploiting our natural resources wasn't even an issue. It seemed as if the earth's bounty was infinite. But in just the last forty years the situation has changed dramatically. Amazingly, in what seems to be a short period of time, we have consumed more natural resources than in the entire prior human history.

---

[2]Silver Ravenwolf, *Teen Witch* (St. Paul: Llewellyn Publications, 2000), 18.
[3]Denise Zimmerman and Katherine A. Gleason, *The Complete Idiot's Guide to Wicca* (Indianapolis, IN: Alpha Books, 2000), 14.
[4]Ibid., 14–15.
[5]Morgan, 32.

Based on the current crisis, some would applaud the Wiccans for trying to do something to help. I, too, give them kudos for wanting to deal with this important issue that affects all of us.

But the problem is with their motivation—to honor mother earth as the living goddess and to nurture and worship her by putting people, plants, animals, and spirit/god all at the same level.

ALL ONE AND ALL EQUAL

In the introduction to the *Teen Witch Datebook,* Wiccan author and elder Raymond Buckland writes, "I also envy you because you are embarking on an exciting journey with incredible rewards. This is a religion and a practice of nature, showing and demonstrating that we are all one and all equal—humans, animals, plants, trees; everything animate and inanimate is closely related."[6] This is beginning to sound a lot like the New Age movement. Is this really an exciting journey, or a dangerous one because of the spiritual deception?

Time magazine calls the New Age "a combination of spirituality and superstition, fad and force, about which the only thing certain is that it is not new." Really, the New Age is nothing but ancient Hinduism and occultism repackaged. Leaders within the movement say it's amazing what you can get people to do when you take away the Hindu and occultic terminology and use language for the twenty-first century.[7]

The New Age can be defined as the growing penetration of Eastern and occultic mysticism into Western culture. The term *New Age* refers to the Aquarian Age, which some New-Agers believe is dawning, bringing with it an era of enlightenment, peace, prosperity, and perfection. Spiritual deception! It's another tool to lure us away from God's truth.

Check out the following two principles found in the New Age movement and see if they don't sound just like Wicca.

1. All is One. One is All. (Monism)

According to New-Agers, every little particle in the universe and every piece of matter everywhere is interconnected. Everything swims

---

[6]Raymond Buckland, *Teen Witch Datebook* (St. Paul: Llewellyn Publications, 2002), 4.
[7]*Time* magazine, December 7, 1987, 62.

in this huge cosmic interconnected ocean. There is no difference between rocks, trees, humans, animals, and God. We are all the same. Allegedly, the reason we have problems in our world today is not because of evil, but ignorance. We are ignorant of the fact that we are all interconnected.

2. God is Everything. Everything is God. (Pantheism)

New-Agers say that everything in creation is part of God—trees, snails, people, etc. Everything has a divine (God-like) nature. It is part of God. The idea of a personal God needs to be abandoned. You don't need a savior because you are *part* of God. If a god (he or she) does exist at all, "it" really exists by chance and is now an impersonal force floating around in the cosmos somewhere.

Sound familiar? Of course, because these are things that Wiccans also believe. These kinds of principles allow Wiccans to worship the creation, mother earth (rocks, sun, moon, etc.), rather than the Creator (God).

Being responsible when it comes to the environment is a value made clear in Scripture, but the Wiccan perspective of worshiping the earth is a reversal of biblical teaching. Let's establish a healthy and God-centered view of caring for the environment, in contrast to the cultural assumption that Christianity promotes the greedy exploitation of creation.

CARETAKERS OF THE PLANET

Wild bird sanctuaries, saving the rainforest, preserving and protecting the Amazon basin, wilderness, wild lands, endangered species—these are all things that God not only cares about but actually created. Let's look at some biblical principles that will enable us to take a healthy approach to dealing with environmental issues. Let's start by getting God's perspective from the Bible, then look at some specific things that we can do to improve the environment. If you're not convinced that you can trust what the Bible says, you may want to jump ahead to the chapter titled "Whose Word You Gonna Trust?" and check out the evidence we have that makes the Bible not only unique but reliable, too.

God is separate from His creation.

God not only created everything, but He holds it all together as well. "In the beginning God created the heavens and the earth" (Genesis 1:1). "Christ is the one through whom God created everything in heaven and earth. He made the things we can see and the things we can't see—kings, kingdoms, rulers, and authorities. Everything has been created through him and for him. He existed before everything else began, and he holds all creation together" (Colossians 1:16–17).

Think about it. If God were a part of creation, He wouldn't be much of a god. He couldn't help us, protect us, and provide for us. And who would hold everything together and keep it from disintegrating into chaos? The balance in nature is a result of God's design. "But God made the earth by his power, and he preserves it by his wisdom. He has stretched out the heavens by his understanding" (Jeremiah 10:12).

People are created in the image of God and are also separate from creation.

In Genesis 1:27 we read, "So God created people in his own image; God patterned them after himself; male and female he created them." From the very beginning the Bible places men and women at the height of God's creation. And neither man nor woman is made more in the image of God than the other.

As people, we are able to think logically, love, forgive, and even set up laws to live by. And most importantly we are able to establish a personal relationship with our Creator. There's no doubt that God loves all that He created (Psalm 65, 104, 145, 147, 148). But the Bible is also very clear that God values people above the critters and creation. Check out the words of Jesus in Matthew 6:26. "Look at the birds. They don't need to plant or harvest or put food in barns because your heavenly Father feeds them. And you are far more valuable to him than they are." If you have time, you should also check out verses 25 and 27–34 of the same chapter. We're not equal with creation, nor are we equal with God. The Bible also tells us that we (humans) are separated from God because of our sin (Romans 3:23).

But because we live in the natural world, we are responsible for how we manage it. The Bible teaches that we were made for relationships—with God, with other people, and with creation—which directly contradicts what Wicca teaches. God is a person, not an impersonal force or an "it." He is alive and is our Lord and Savior. The Bible is filled with His characteristics, and they tell us what kind of a great and awesome God He really is (Deuteronomy 6:4; Ephesians 1:3).

Problems with the environment started a long time ago.

It's hard to believe that the environmental crises actually started way back at the beginning of human history. Adam and Eve—the first man and woman—lived in paradise to start with. The Garden of Eden was like heaven on earth—everything was perfect. They would have lived there forever if they had not disobeyed God. But they were deceived by Satan—disguised as a serpent—and became convinced that their way was better than God's. They sinned and fell from God's loving presence (Genesis 3:1–7).

Adam and Eve's choice to disobey God affected all of creation, including the environment.

> And to Adam he said, "Because you listened to your wife and ate the fruit I told you not to eat, I have placed a curse on the ground. All your life you will struggle to scratch a living from it. It will grow thorns and thistles for you, though you will eat of its grains." (Genesis 3:17–18)

And just like Adam and Eve, all of us have sinned and have a broken relationship with God (Romans 3:23). Previous generations didn't think anything about small choices they made environmentally, like dumping garbage in streams and polluting them. Now we know that just small amounts of garbage in a large quantity of water can be hazardous to human health. That's why it's so important that we learn that choices have consequences, and our consequences can affect people in other parts of the world and in future generations. The horrible environmental problems we see today are because of the continued sinful actions of people.

God is going to make a new earth.

There's no doubt that the world is physically decaying. Things are definitely getting worse, and we need to do what we can to make changes where possible that will slow down this process. Earth as we know it will not last forever, but there will be a new one created (Revelation 21:1). It will all be according to God's plan and timetable.

> Against its will, everything on earth was subjected to God's curse. All creation anticipates the day when it will join God's children in glorious freedom from death and decay. For we know that all creation has been groaning as in the pains of childbirth right up to the present time. (Romans 8:20–22)

It's interesting to realize that creation and our fate are tied closely together. And both will experience restoration and a bringing together of God with His creation.

We don't have to be bummed out or paranoid, because God has promised to make a new earth and heaven. We also have the hope of being completely transformed by God's power. We won't be reincarnated or recycled. There will be no more sickness, cancer, or AIDS because we will have new bodies. God already started this process spiritually when Jesus died on the cross to pay the penalty for our sin.

God has commissioned all of us to use our creative abilities to make earth a better place to live. As we serve God, we should do everything we can to manage all of creation in the best way possible.

So what can we practically do?

When it comes to the earth and our environment, God wants us to manage and enjoy the things He created. Look at Genesis 1:28–30 (also see 9:1–3).

> God blessed them and told them, "Multiply and fill the earth and subdue it. Be masters over the fish and birds and all the animals." And God said, "Look! I have given you the seed-bearing plants throughout the earth and all the fruit trees for your food. And I have given all the grasses and other green plants to the animals and birds for their food."

This is a huge responsibility that we don't always take very seriously. Think about it—God gave us the earth and all its awesome beauty to enjoy. All He asks us to do in return is honor Him by taking care of it. He's put us in charge of developing all the potential He put into the natural world. We are caretakers of His garden! (Genesis 2:15).

But we need to start by having the right attitude so we can take the right action. Having the right attitude means that we recognize God as the Creator and that we are dependent on Him, as well as the fruitfulness of creation, for our health and survival. He is the one who keeps everything functioning and in order.

> You cause grass to grow for the cattle. You cause plants to grow for people to use. You allow them to produce food from the earth—wine to make them glad, olive oil as lotion for their skin, and bread to give them strength.
>
> The trees of the LORD are well cared for—the cedars of Lebanon that he planted. There the birds make their nests, and the storks make their homes in the firs. High in the mountains are pastures for the wild goats, and the rocks form a refuge for rock badgers.
>
> You made the moon to mark the seasons and the sun that knows when to set. You send the darkness, and it becomes night, when all the forest animals prowl about. Then the young lions roar for their food, but they are dependent on God. (Psalm 104:14–21)

We must also recognize that God thinks highly of His creation and has compassion for it (Genesis 1:31). For that reason we have to pay close attention to our choices and consequences—sowing and reaping (Galatians 6:7). How we live, what we eat, what we buy, and the amount of garbage we produce all has an effect on the strain caused in the natural world. We need to keep the "big picture" in mind and think about the long-term impact of our "footprints" on the environment, others, and future generations. Our lifestyle should encourage conservation and good stewardship rather than abuse.

With the right attitude and motivation you can make a difference that will not only affect you but future generations as well. And remember, God is the One who deserves our worship and our love. We can respect creation because He designed it and gave it life. Why would you want to worship rocks, trees, planets, and other created things when you can love and adore the Master Builder and experience His love, care, provision, and unlimited power?

The challenge we face is to use the land, resources, our lives, and our time in such a way that honors God and helps others. Ultimately, God is the rightful owner of the earth and all that it contains (Psalm 24:1). We are servants in charge of the Master's property, and one day we will have to answer for what we've done with it (Matthew 25:14–30; Luke 12:47, 16:1–2; Romans 14:12).

CHAPTER SEVEN:
A SENSE OF BELONGING

LORD FARQUAAD RULED OVER the kingdom of Duloc and was determined that it would be perfect. But the kingdom was filled with fairy-tale characters and he didn't want them around. He even offered rewards to get rid of them. Finally they were all rounded up and sent off to the swamp.

Farquaad's ultimate desire was to be king of Duloc. But he found out in order to become king, he had to marry a princess. Lord Farquaad knew of a beautiful princess named Fiona and decided that she would be a perfect queen. Unfortunately, Fiona was living in a castle, guarded by a dragon. The only way the princess could be rescued was to defeat the dragon. So Lord Farquaad devised a plan to send someone else to rescue Fiona. That's where Shrek comes in.

Shrek isn't your typical hero. In most animated fairy tales the hero is a prince. But Shrek is a large green ogre who lives alone in a swamp. He's grumpy at times but also has a softer side. Shrek likes being a loner, but one day he meets Donkey—a talking donkey—who has escaped from Lord Farquaad's guards. Donkey seems to like Shrek, who just wants to be left alone.

Shrek is furious when fairy-tale characters invade his swamp. Off he goes—with Donkey following him—to see Lord Farquaad to find out how to get his swamp back. Lord Farquaad informs Shrek he can have his swamp back on the condition that he rescues Princess Fiona. So off he goes to the castle.

Princess Fiona had been waiting for a long time to be rescued, and Shrek wasn't the kind of hero she expected. But Fiona had a secret that no one knew about—she turns into an ogre every day when the sun sets. Fiona quickly got over her initial surprise of her ogre rescuer, and she and Shrek became friends. This was all new to Shrek; he wasn't used to being around others. First Donkey, now Fiona, and he begins to open up just a little bit. But after an unfortunate misunderstanding, Shrek closes up once again.

The struggle to belong and be accepted continues in the first block-buster movie. Shrek isn't sure that he can be accepted because he's an ogre, and Fiona doesn't know if she will be loved and accepted because of her secret. Eventually they find themselves in love and they marry. The movie is all about being loved for who you are on the inside, rather than how you look on the outside. It's about belonging and identity.

Let's face it—we all want to belong. We want people to like us. We want to feel significant. This was a big struggle for me as a teenager. I had a horrible self-image—I hated myself. I would stand at my locker and curse God for making me look the way I did. Besides being tall and skinny—my nickname was "Sticks" because I played drums and because of my legs—I had dark, curly hair. It was your basic 'Fro. I wanted straight blond hair. Unfortunately, my parents wouldn't let me bleach my hair, so I tried everything I could think of to straighten it. Hair gel didn't work, and blow-drying it only made it worse. I also had two fangs sticking practically straight out of my mouth. When I laughed or smiled, I covered my mouth with my hand because I was so embarrassed.

The worst thing of all was my mother's fault. I'm convinced my mom gave birth to a five-pound nose and my body grew off of it!

I was desperate for relationships. I wanted to fit in and feel like I belonged. But I didn't think anyone else could like me unless I was sitting behind a set of drums. The drums became my life, my security, my significance.

Sound familiar? Teens place huge value on belonging to a particular "tribe." This is their circle of closest friends—kind of like a family. There are many different subcultures that exist today, and most people belong to more than one. Look around your school and you'll see the different subcultures your peers identify with: boarders, Goths, geeks, Jesus freaks . . . and more.

Identity has always been a huge concern for teens. Today's subculture battles are not about turf and respect, they are efforts to define themselves and be set apart to belong to a "tribe" of like-minded peers. Things like clothing styles, tattoos, and body piercings are symbols of core values that associate someone with a particular subculture.

And for some, no matter what you do, you just don't belong—and that hurts. Everyone has been hurt by others, but that hurt is especially damaging when it comes at the hands of those who say they're Christians. Take shock-rocker Marilyn Manson, for example.

Manson was raised in the Episcopal Church and went to a non-denominational Christian school. But he never really fit in and got picked on a lot for being different. Now he says he identifies with Satan. "So that was the point where I started to seek out other interpretations of God. And initially, when you rebel, you go for the obvious choices—heavy metal, Satanism. To me, Satan ultimately represents rebellion. Lucifer was the angel that was kicked out of heaven because he wanted to be God. To me, what greater character to identify with?"[1]

If Christians are seen as being elite, judgmental, two-faced, and phony, it's easy to seek an alternative religion that won't demand conforming to an illogical external standard of dress or appearance. Wicca provides that sense of acceptance.

But the question is: By what and by whom? To start with, many who practice Wicca are solitaries—individuals who prefer to practice the craft on their own, working out their rituals privately and pacing their spiritual journey as they see fit.[2] Then there's the nebulous All and the god and the goddess, and of course the deities a Wiccan creates.

Do you feel like you belong and really know who you are? This is another area of spiritual deception that we sometimes fail to recognize.

[1] www.beliefnet.com.
[2] Michele Morgan, Simple Wicca (Berkeley: Conari Press, 2000), 24.

If the devil can keep us confused about our true identity, he'll keep us frustrated, lacking confidence, and we will not experience a satisfying and fulfilling life.

Knowing who you are is the key to a meaningful life. When we come to grips with who we are, our whole perspective on life radically changes. But many people don't know how to find their identity (it takes more than a magical incantation or spell!), and when they do, they often don't want to believe it. They're afraid they might have to become someone they don't really want to be.

Identity—security, significance, and acceptance—can only be found in a personal relationship with God through His Son, Jesus.

HOW NOT TO DETERMINE WHO YOU ARE

Telling me your name, where you live, where you go to school, or what you like to do are things about you. But even with all that information, you still haven't told me who you really are.

Who we are is not determined by what we do, where we live, where we go to school, or even the stuff we possess. I met a high school guy who introduced himself to me and immediately told me all about the brand-new Mustang convertible his dad had just bought him. This guy went on and on for more than twenty minutes talking about his car. He told me every possible detail imaginable!

I wanted to interrupt him. "Time out! Are you trying to tell me who you are, or about something you own? I'm confused."

When I was in high school I did well in academics and sports, but my passion was music. It was my life. So when I went to my high school class reunion, people thought I was still doing the music gig. They would come up and say, "Hey, Russo. Who are you playing with and recording with now?" When I responded that I was now in full-time ministry, they didn't know what to say. It was almost as if I'd told them I had some strange tropical disease that was highly contagious. They politely said "bye" and walked away. All through high school everybody had my identity wrapped up in the drums. And so did I.

The confusion over identity can work the opposite way as well. If you can't perform or you don't have the status or possessions society says you need, you may start thinking of yourself as worthless. You may see yourself as a loser because you didn't make good grades in a certain class or you didn't make the team. Or maybe you've heard from your parents, teachers, or even friends for a long time that you'll never succeed in anything.

I took a speech/communication class my freshman year of college. One day after class the professor asked to speak with me privately. "Mr. Russo, there's one thing I want to encourage you never to consider as a profession—public speaking. You can't speak clearly. Your mannerisms are bad. You just don't have what it takes." That's strange, isn't it? Today I speak to audiences all over the world: face-to-face and on the radio and TV! I'd like to find that professor now and let her see what God can do in a person's life.

Have you discovered your identity? Who you are is determined by much more than what you have, what you do, and what you achieve. Just ask Keith Wegemen.

DISCOVERING WHO YOU ARE

As far back as he could remember, Keith's main goal in life was to make the Olympic ski team. Finally in 1952 he was chosen for the Olympics. After months of practice, Keith headed to Europe for the games. The day finally came when he was to experience the greatest thrill of his life. There he stood at the top of the world's highest ski jump at Oberstdorf, Germany.

For a moment, he paused all alone, 650 feet above the outrun of the jump. The eighty thousand people below him seemed no bigger than ants. Then the signal was given and the crowd was silent as he plummeted down at over eighty miles per hour. His senses couldn't keep up with the scream of the wind and the blur of trees, snow, and sky. Then suddenly he was hanging motionless over the white hill below. After what seemed like an eternity, Keith landed sixteen feet beyond the four-hundred-foot mark—the longest jump an American skier had ever made up to that time.

Two weeks later Keith was on a plane headed back to New York. The Olympics were over. Now what? As the engines droned on endlessly, somewhere over the Atlantic the thought hit him: *What, then, does last? What's important in the long run? What's the answer?* He was twenty-three years old and had never thought about these questions before. Once he arrived home, he couldn't seem to find any thrills that would last—they all wore thin quickly, even with the celebrity status he now had with all the endorsements and appearances.

Sometime later he was visiting his brother and some friends in Southern California. They invited him to attend a young adults' conference in the San Bernardino Mountains. He attended a few of the meetings but spent most of his time swimming, climbing, and hiking. Still, Keith decided he'd better make an appearance at the closing meeting. The auditorium was hot and he didn't really listen too much, until the speaker was toward the end of his message and started talking about pleasures in this life that don't last. Keith sat straight up in his chair when he heard the speaker say, "What, then, does last? What's important in the long run? What's the answer?" He couldn't believe his ears. Those were the same questions he asked himself while flying over the Atlantic.

"Do you want to know the answer?" the speaker continued. Keith bent forward in his chair and heard, "Try Jesus." He jumped up and ran outside toward the safety of the mountain. After an hour, he finally stopped, sat down on a slope, and let the words he'd been running from catch up to him. He had known about Jesus as an idea or principle, but now he would know Him as a person. Keith's life would never be the same. Now he had a different kind of thrill to live for—one that wouldn't wear thin.

Keith found out what everyone on this planet needs to know: You become complete as a person and have a life of meaning and purpose when you find your identity in Jesus. This happens when we surrender our lives and put our faith and trust in Him.

It's only in Jesus that we find out who we really are. And that's what finally happened to Keith. He was confronted with the truth and came to love the One who knew him better than anyone else—even better than he knew himself. Keith found out about the One who put him together, piece by piece, molecule by molecule, in his mother's womb. In Jesus his true identity was found. And this knowledge totally transformed Keith Wegemen's life.

How about you? Have you come to grips with who you are in Jesus? Do you realize that He loves you just the way you are? You're somebody special in His eyes. Billions of people have been born and walked the face of this planet, yet there has never been any two who are exactly alike—not even identical twins. I want you to read something that describes this fact perfectly. It's called *I'm Special* and that famous author, Anonymous, wrote it. After you read it, take some time to really let the message soak in.

I'M SPECIAL

I'm special. In all the world there's nobody like me. Since the beginning of time, there has never been another person like me. Nobody has my smile. Nobody has my eyes, my nose, my hair, my hands, my voice. I'm special.

No one can be found who has my handwriting. Nobody anywhere has my tastes—for food or music or art. No one sees things just as I do. In all of time there's been no one who laughs like me, no one who cries like me. And what makes me laugh and cry will never provoke identical laughter and tears from anybody else, ever. No one reacts to any situation just as I would react. I'm special.

I'm the only one in all of creation who has my set of abilities. Oh, there will always be somebody who is better at one of the things I'm good at, but no one in the universe can reach my combination of talents, ideas, abilities, and feelings. Like a room full of musical instruments, some may excel alone, but none can match the symphony sound when all are played together. I'm a symphony.

Through all of eternity no one will ever look, talk, walk, think, or do like me. I'm special. I'm rare.

And in all rarity there is great value. Because of my great, rare value, I need not attempt to imitate others. I will accept—yes, celebrate—my differences. I'm special.

And I'm beginning to realize it's no accident that I'm special.

I'm beginning to see that God made me special for a very special purpose.

He must have a job for me that no one else can do as well as I. Out of all the billions of applicants, only one is qualified, only one has the right combination of what it takes.

That one is me. Because . . . I'm special.[3]

This is just the start. Now that you're beginning to realize how special you really are, let's take a closer look at how to begin developing your true identity.

YOUR TRUE IDENTITY

In the Bible we learn that when you establish a relationship with Jesus Christ, you have a new life. "What this means is that those who become Christians become new persons. They are not the same anymore, for the old life is gone. A new life has begun!" (2 Corinthians 5:17). When you put your faith and trust in Jesus, you become a brand-new person, a person who didn't exist before. Ephesians 5:8 says, "For you were once darkness, but now you are light in the Lord. Live as children of light" (NIV). There isn't anything more dramatically different than darkness and light. This is how different your life will be once you recognize who you are in Jesus.

This concept is often misunderstood today, so let's clear up some of the confusion. To begin with, did you know that there are two births you can have in life? A physical one and a spiritual one. When you are born physically, the result is physical life. When you are re-born spiritually, you receive eternal life.

When you are born spiritually, it opens up all the other dimensions of your life—social, emotional, physical, intellectual—enabling you to become the person God designed you to be. All of a sudden life starts to make sense. A new life in Christ gives you a brand-new identity. Becoming a Christian is not just something you add to your life—it's something that becomes your life. You may look the same on the outside, but you're a radically different person on the inside.

---

[3]Author unknown.

As a brand-new person, God also gives you a new heart. You have been completely forgiven of all your sin and given a new start at life. That means you can stop living under the cloud of guilt about your past. Start experiencing life as the person God designed you to be. The penalty for your sin has been paid in full by Jesus dying on the cross. And you've been given an awesome new power to overcome the difficulties in life as well. The power you now have available to you is the same power that brought Jesus back to life from the grave on the very first Easter Sunday. It's called resurrection power, and it's available to help with all the pain and difficult issues in your life. This power never runs out, and you can only get it from the living God of the Bible.

Life isn't always easy, especially in today's world. Broken families, money problems, unrealistic expectations, abuse, and stress can get you down. Things get even more complicated when you add the spiritual battle that is raging in your life. Don't get too overwhelmed. Learn to trust God. Take it one step at a time. When you learn to rely on Him with the small things, it will be easier when dealing with the big stuff.

There's a promise found in Jeremiah 29:11. "'For I know the plans I have for you,' says the Lord. 'They are plans for good and not for disaster, to give you a future and a hope.'" God wants you to get the most out of life. When you have secured your eternal destiny and identity through Christ, it should affect the quality of life you live here on earth. There will always be problems, pressures, and struggles, but the way you respond is going to be much different because now you have all the resources of the living God giving you power to enable you to face the challenges head on.

It's extremely important to recognize that you're not the same person you once were after you have a relationship with Jesus. If you're thinking to yourself, *I have accepted Jesus and I'm still struggling with my identity and my self-image*, then you're still being deceived. The devil has distorted the truth about your identity. Stop listening to his lies and start living God's truth. Satan would like you to believe that nothing's really changed, but God no longer sees us as we once were.

God changes us so completely in Christ that even He looks at us differently. "For we are God's masterpiece. He has created us anew in Christ Jesus, so that we can do the good things he planned for us long ago" (Ephesians 2:10). Since God considers us His masterpieces, we shouldn't treat ourselves or others as junk or with disrespect.

Meaning and purpose that lasts throughout life cannot be found outside of Jesus. Stop wandering down the empty, experiential, psychic path of Wicca. If you have a relationship with God through Jesus, you are a child of God. Check this out: "But to all who believed him and accepted him, he gave the right to become children of God" (John 1:12). Since our Father in heaven is the Lord of lords and the King of kings, what does that make us? Children of the King. Talk about significant! Are you living like the royalty that you truly are?

Paul challenges us to live lives worthy of who we are in Ephesians 4:1. "Therefore I, as a prisoner for serving the Lord, beg you to lead a life worthy of your calling, for you have been called by God." What happens when Prince Charles of England goes anywhere? How is he treated? People literally roll out the red carpet for him. Heads of State and bands greet him. People take extra special care of him. He even has bodyguards for protection. Why? Because he is royalty and the future king of England.

But if you are a follower of Jesus, you have a much greater heritage and inheritance than Prince Charles. You are a child of the King of the heavens and you will rule forever with the Lord of all creation.

HOW GOD DESCRIBES WHO WE ARE

The Bible is filled with incredible descriptions of our identity in Jesus Christ. Let's take a look at some of the verses that can help us get an even better idea of who we really are.

In 1 Corinthians 6:19–20 we read: "Don't you know that your body is the temple of the Holy Spirit, who lives in you and was given to you by God? You do not belong to yourself, for God bought you with a high price. So you must honor God with your body." What was the cost of buying your freedom from the powers of darkness? It was the very life of God's only Son, Jesus. God paid the highest price possible so your relationship with Him could be restored and your true identity secured. Isn't it amazing how valuable you are to God and how much He loves you?

Knowing that we were bought with such a tremendous price should cause us to be more careful with the things that we get involved in. You don't have to "loan yourself out" and sell out your values to things like sex before marriage, gangs, or even abusing drugs and alcohol just to feel worth something or escape the pain. There's no reason to compromise any longer to get someone to love you. God will provide for all your needs. You were bought with the ultimate price, so live like it and don't settle for anything less.

Colossians 1:13 describes the security that is part of our identity: "For he has rescued us from the one who rules in the kingdom of darkness, and he has brought us into the Kingdom of his dear Son." Before we accepted Christ, you and I were hostages of the devil to do his will (2 Timothy 2:26). We were prisoners, but God set us free! And Jesus said that once we are His, no one can take us from Him (John 10:28).

Do you remember the response of some of the Iraqi citizens after the Coalition forces, as part of Operation Iraqi Freedom, had liberated their city? There was dancing in the streets, people hugging each other, and in some cases Iraqi men even wanted to kiss the soldiers for setting them free! The celebrations were fantastic. It seemed like a lot of people in the world partied.

But did you know that there is an even greater celebration for those who are set free from Satan's prison? Check out the words of Jesus in Luke 15:7: "In the same way, heaven will be happier over one lost sinner who returns to God than over ninety-nine others who are righteous and haven't strayed away!" When someone accepts Jesus Christ, it's party time in heaven! Spiritual freedom through Jesus is secure and lasts forever.

Next time you're feeling insecure because friends have rejected you or because of a tough family situation, stop and think about your security in Christ. Let this knowledge about your true identity influence your behavior. There's no need to fear anyone or anything that life may throw at you. "For God has not given us a spirit of fear and timidity, but of power, love, and self-discipline" (2 Timothy 1:7). Having a relationship with Jesus really can make a difference in the way you live.

Isn't it amazing how many dimensions of life our identity (or lack of it) affects?

With Jesus we have everything we'll ever need to make life worth living. That's not to say we don't need other relationships or a fulfilling career, but without knowing who we are in Christ, everything else is meaningless. "How we praise God, the Father of our Lord Jesus Christ, who has blessed us with every spiritual blessing in the heavenly realms because we belong to Christ" (Ephesians 1:3). Our minds can't even begin to comprehend what God has blessed us with or what He has planned for us to experience (1 Corinthians 2:9). Don't miss what you can experience through Jesus by continuing to search for something more in the deception and emptiness of Wicca.

KNOWING WHO WE ARE AFFECTS HOW WE ACT

If we could really grasp what our identity in Christ means in our day-to-day experiences, I'm convinced that we'd see some of the problems that plague us shrink and maybe even disappear altogether.

Whether it's sex outside of marriage, drug and alcohol abuse, bullying or gangs, the answer is the same—Jesus.

I could fill pages with youth-culture issues that have their roots in the problem of identity. We could talk about eating disorders, suicidal tendencies, and people who cut themselves, and we'd keep coming back to the fact that knowing who we are affects how we act. I don't want to sound overly simplistic, but so many problems today could be solved by helping people find their true identity and letting that influence the way they live.

Some of the most frequent questions teens ask me are, "Give me a reason to get up in the morning," "Why am I here?" "How can I make a difference with my life?" All of these questions and more can be answered in one word—Jesus. Whether you want to admit it or not, Satan will try to deceive you into not believing this awesome truth. He started doing this back in the beginning of human history with the first man and woman—Adam and Eve—and he hasn't changed his strategy since. Deception is his greatest weapon, especially when it comes to our identity. Satan knows all too well that the truth about who you are is the thing that will set you free. Jesus said, "I am the way and the truth and the life" (John 14:6). Lasting security, acceptance, and significance will only be found in Christ.

You're not going to find your identity, security, significance, and acceptance in a force called the All or by worshiping the earth. And you'll never find your identity, security, significance, and acceptance in deities you've designed and made yourself. Wicca is a deceptive, empty, man-made religion.

The only place you are going to find your real identity is in a vital, intimate relationship with Jesus Christ. This happens by surrendering your heart and life to Him and saying, "Jesus, I want you to invade my humanity and help me to become the person I was designed to be so I can experience a rich and satisfying life."

It's not a spell, ritual, or incantation that will help you find yourself. It's through surrendering your life—an act of your will—to the living God of the Bible. When you find yourself in Him, your life will never be the same.

CHAPTER EIGHT

BUILD YOUR OWN RELIGION

PAUL'S YOUR AVERAGE TEENAGE GUY who has some strong opinions when it comes to religion. "Religion is like anything else—you do what you like. Take music, for instance—you wouldn't listen to jazz if you preferred rock. Religion wasn't invented to create supremacy. It leaves me speechless how closed-minded and brainwashed people in religious groups can be. I'm my own free spirit. My Holy Bible, my Koran, my Bhagavad Gita[1]—my set of morals I thought of on my own. I didn't need a book and I am still a good person. In fact, I know a lot more bad Christians than I know bad 'undecided' people."

Sound familiar? I'll bet you know a lot of people on your campus with similar views. We live in a culture where truth is relative and it's trendy to custom-design your own belief system and morality. Everyone seems to be doing it. I was online and checked out an ongoing

---

[1] Probably the most famous and widely read ethical text of ancient India, the Bhagavad Gita now ranks as one of the three principal texts that define and capture the essence of Hinduism, the other two being the Upanishads and the Brahma Sutras.

forum chat about "Christian witchcraft." Here's some of the discussion that was taking place:

- "I figure since a lot of pagans use different gods and goddesses, then why not just use 'God' or JC? Maybe incorporate some saints? Or even angels? I haven't used them in any of my magickal works yet, but I plan to. There are some great angel spells out there like a guardian angel spell which is seemingly really easy." GT

- "I look at it that God doesn't care what you believe, just that you do, and that belief kind of revolves around what are, for me at least, universal truths of decent behavior. You don't lie to each other. You don't steal from each other. You respect your elders (even if you don't like them, because everyone has something to teach even if it's only 'Don't do this'). You don't kill people just to kill them. You celebrate life and the beauty it entails and try to learn to be appreciative that you have been given the opportunity to experience it, regardless of how many times you may have." DH

- "Regarding the 'no other gods' commandment and its application to things 'occulty'—the commandment is that 'thou shall have no gods before me.' In the Hebrew Scriptures, there seems to be recognition of a plurality of gods—but that none of them are to be worshipped by the Hebrew peoples. Whether or not other gods are a reality is not necessarily covered by the commandment. The commandment enjoins its adherents not to place any of them (gods)— regardless of whether or not they exist—before God. Ultimately, I take the relationship between 'thou shall have no other gods' and esoteric practice, whether it be magic(k) or mysticism, to be an injunction not to put anything before God. John of the Cross writes about the danger of seeking visions and mystical experiences—for him it was putting the experience and the vision before the relationship with God. There is no reality apart from the Reality, no existence apart from the Existence. When you abandon reality in favor of Reality, you gain the All. For the righteous man there is no law— he has become a law unto himself." DV

- "Did you notice that in the Bible it says do not have any other gods before me? It doesn't say that there isn't any; just don't have them before him or her or it. Therefore, I am under the assumption that there are many gods, deities/saints, and other higher beings or wherever they are. Just don't worship them over him, meaning don't pick them over me.

  "Personally when I started to practice magick I started with witchcraft. Loved it but couldn't get around all of the gods and goddesses that were being called to aid them in their work or help them, etc. That is my Christian side coming out. So I was conflicted for a while, thinking what do I do, how do I get around this obstacle and still practice magick. I didn't like calling on the divine, even Christian divinity, saints, etc. I felt and still feel now that all they are—divine beings, gods, servants [sic]. All they do is provide much concentrated energy when called upon by a mage or witch. Of course, it is more powerful because it's more concentrated and coming from a divine being, but energy is all around us, we can raise enough to get the same results they do. It might take longer and take experience and practice, but we can all do it. So I started to get into energy magick. Raising energy to do my spells and not calling on the divine. It has worked pretty d——n good too. But lately I've been exploring my spiritual side, I feel I've suppressed it a lot. So I just might start calling on divine beings, mending my relationship with god. But I will still be able to fall back on my other talents, energy magic and what not. This is just a new road for me, one I hope will lead me to a very spiritual life, and a magical one at that too." GM

- "I am just learning how to do this stuff. I'm trying to contact my great-great-grandma Clara, so that I can learn of things she used. She used the power of the divine to heal and to accomplish many tasks. She would never take money. I recognize that other gods do exist, and they have their places in the universe. But there is one god at the top of the hierarchy for me." JJ

- "There was a time in my life when I referred to myself as a Christian witch. I no longer do so because I feel it is inaccurate in light of my beliefs, though they have changed very little. At the beginning of this year, I was baptized by water. It was necessary, as I did not feel I would be physically capable of leaving the sanctuary until I made that commitment to Christ, whose name I was using to describe my personal belief system. I am glad I did it. It was one of the most honest things I have ever done. I have accepted Jesus as my teacher and savior, for he has saved me from the mire of my own arrogance and ignorance. I follow his teachings to the best of my ability. I regard the rest of the Bible as a valuable reference on theological history, just as I regard all other religious texts.

  "These days I make no claims to be anything other than an energy witch. I have had to admit to myself that I do not genuinely believe in any ALL-powerful being, and I am therefore certainly not a Christian in any sort of the accepted sense. Faith is a marvelous gift—one I hold in high regard. I do believe that a true faith in any thing lends validity to that thing's existence and empowers it." KA

- "Prayer is like doubt. You must doubt the power of your god if you have to pray to him—it—to solve your problems. You can accomplish much more for yourself through meditation and chakra work, more than any bible or 'god' could help you." PC

- "Using aspects of Christianity is not in direct conflict with Witchcraft, unless you interpret that. They have miracles, we have outcomes. They have prayers, we have spells. It's all in the interpretation. I do not fear that I'm going to hell, because I am not Christian. But there are aspects of Christianity that can be incorporated into Witchcraft. I also don't believe that if you are a Christian that practices Witchcraft (which is not an oxymoron) that you will automatically go to hell." LD

- "I don't believe that god wants to crucify witches and he hates them, etc. He gave us free will to do what we want. He doesn't want to hurt you or d——n you because you pursued another spiritual path. As long as you're not hurting anyone and you are being spiritual yourself, even though it might not be through him, I think he thinks it is all right." SX

It's all about building your own religion based on feelings, opinions, and experiences. In addition to having the choice to make up your own set of morals, Wicca also gives its followers the freedom to pick and choose what to believe and what to reject. Its billing as one of the most flexible religions out there is based on its allowance for contradictory beliefs and is often desirable for those who prefer a self-styled religion in a reality of their making.

HAVE IT YOUR WAY

A popular fast-food restaurant chain tells its customers, "Have it your way." Wicca tells its followers the same thing. Maybe that's why it's so hard to define Wicca. There's some people who claim to be Wiccans who use the terms "Wicca" and "witchcraft" interchangeably. Then there are groups within witchcraft who follow the Wicca variety. Finally, there's the group that makes a distinction between Wicca and witchcraft. Wiccans dislike any attempt to standardize their beliefs.

Wicca is a "buffet-style" religion and in a sense gives followers the freedom to be their own god. It also appeals to human pride and natural rebellious spirit. According to mega-selling Wiccan author Scott Cunningham, there is not and can never be one "pure" or "true" or "genuine" form of Wicca. There are no central governing agencies, no physical leaders, no universally recognized prophets or messengers. Although specific, structured forms of Wicca certainly exist, they aren't in agreement regarding ritual, symbolism, and theology. Because of this "healthy" individualism, no one ritual or philosophical system has emerged to consume the others.[2]

Wicca, the religion of witches, is so self-styled that it's tough to get agreement on the exact and original meaning of the word *Wicca*. But this hasn't stopped teens from getting into the craft. It's a seemingly

---

[2]Scott Cunningham, *Wicca: A Guide for the Solitary Practitioner* (St. Paul: Llewellyn Publications, 2003), xi.

perfect fit for those who want a personally involving religion, celebrating both physical and spiritual realities, in which getting connected with deity is attached with the practice of magick. Most Wiccans or witches tend to worship nature, are experience oriented, do not believe in absolutes, and believe in many gods.

A big part of the attraction of the craft is the freedom to choose whom to worship. Naming a god is about what "works for you" spiritually. Some have compared the idea of Wiccan deities to a family tree (or pyramid), with the All, or universal energy, or "One" at the top. The All/One is basically a huge melting pot of all the gods everyone in the world has ever thought of or believed in.

The All/One is not male or female, has no body or real personality. It's more like a blender that you've dumped all the beliefs of the world into and crushed together. Travel down the pyramid, and the All/One divides into two halves—female and male. The lord and the lady (god and goddess) symbolize the perfectly balanced male and female aspects of divinity that is vital to most Wiccans. Finally, closest to humans on earth, are the gods and goddesses. And just like you might choose a friend based on things that appeal to you instinctively or emotionally, so can Wiccans choose their favorite traits for a god and goddess.

There's no set of guidelines that dictates who or what the god and goddess must be; rather, there are ancient and symbolic descriptions of their essences and energies. The rest is left up to the individual Wiccans to design. The god can be tough or tender, fair-skinned or dark, long hair or short—whatever physicalities are desired.

But it doesn't stop here. There are also additional gods and goddesses that belong to a specific "pantheon" or group of deities that serve a particular people or culture, which a Wiccan can also add to their personal belief system. Some of the more common goddesses in Wicca are Aphrodite, Aradia, Bast, and Demeter. A few of the more common gods are Cernunnos, Horus, Mithra, and Taleisin.

Psychic Michele Morgan, in her book *Simple Wicca*, says it's all about personal responsibility. "There's no confession or absolution of sins by an outside authority. Instead Wiccans are required to face up to their own actions, admit their mistakes and set things right whenever they can. Wiccans also believe in reincarnation, which deepens their commitment to personal and spiritual growth and to learning from all experiences."[3]

The craft encourages followers to develop a personal religious practice, gleaned from one's own experiences, wisdom, and instincts. Wiccans respect the idea that different spiritual beliefs work for different people. In fact, many witches add aspects of other religious systems, such as Native American Shamanism or Buddhism, to their rituals and practices. Others work closely with saints, angels, and even try to put Jesus into the mix. Religion is the language of spirituality, and Wiccans are definitely multilingual.[4]

The "cool" thing about Wicca is that there's no one right way to practice, worship, or believe. It's all about finding what fits for the individual—choosing what works for them spiritually—what they like, relate to, and identify with. Wicca is all about the individual and being in control of one's own destiny.

THE ONLY TRUE GOD

Surrender isn't a very popular word nowadays. Take, for example, all the hot spots globally where fighting is taking place. Neither side wants to surrender, because that means they will lose. Or how about out on the highway—surrendering the right-of-way to another car? Are you kidding? Even if we're sitting in bumper-to-bumper traffic, something inside us says, "Don't give in to the car that's trying to merge in traffic from an on-ramp." But sometimes you don't have much choice when it comes to surrendering.

I travel a lot, which means I fly on quite a few airplanes. Every time I get on a plane I'm basically surrendering my life to the pilot. He or she is in charge of getting me where I need to go. There's no debating with him or her on which route I think they should take. When I step on that plane, I have decided to put my trust in that pilot to get me safely to my destination. And I have to admit there have been times that I've wondered if I made the right choice to trust a particular pilot—especially on some overseas flights. After one especially scary

---

[3]Michele Morgan, *Simple Wicca* (Berkeley: Conari Press, 2000), 9.
[4]Ibid., 11–12.

flight, as I was walking off the plane, the pilot smiled and said, "Cheated death once again!" That's not want you want to hear a pilot say!

Isn't it crazy how many times a week we put our trust in something or someone? When was the last time you tested your burger or burrito to see if it had been laced with poison? Or how about the chair you're sitting in—did you test it before you sat down to see if it would hold you? Unless you're really paranoid, you rarely stop to think about these kinds of things. So why is it so easy to surrender our will and put our trust in so many other people and things and not in God?

There are lots of reasons, but here are a few specific ones. First, you can't physically see God. But think about this: Have you ever seen the wind? Of course not, but you know it's there and you see the effects of it. Then there's the whole attitude of society that basically encourages us to be control freaks, especially when it comes to spirituality. But there is something else you may not have thought about—spiritual warfare and the devil. Wiccans say he doesn't exist, that he's a concept Christians have made up. But that isn't historically or biblically accurate. Think about it: If the devil is real, and he is our enemy, he definitely wouldn't want you to surrender your life to God and trust Him.

Wicca is leading a lot of teens—even those who attend church—down an empty and deceptive spiritual path. When you try to build your own religion and make your own gods, you put yourself in a dangerous position. What good is your religion or your god if they're no bigger than you? You're going to run out of energy, your wisdom is limited, as well as your personal resources. Whom do you turn to for help when your back is up against the wall? And how about love and forgiveness? How can you experience love from the moon, a rock, or some nebulous "universal energy" out in the cosmos somewhere? Or how about dealing with guilt? Wicca offers no real answers for any of these questions and more.

Habakkuk was a man who lived a long time ago in the Middle East. He had many of the same tough questions that we face today. And he wanted answers, just like you and I, so he boldly took his questions straight to God. And God answered him. Here's an answer Habakkuk received that speaks directly to Wicca and making up your own religion.

> What have you gained by worshiping all your man-made idols? How foolish to trust in something made by your own hands! What fools you are to believe such lies! How terrible it will be for you who beg lifeless wooden idols to save you. You ask speechless stone images to tell you what to do. Can an idol speak for God? They may be overlaid with gold and silver, but they are lifeless inside. (Habakkuk 2:18–19)

It doesn't get any clearer than that!

We don't really talk a lot about idolatry today, but it's more than just bowing down to some figurine or statue; it's trusting in what you've made and therefore in your own power as creator and sustainer. Do you trust in God or what your hands have made? Idols have no life, no personhood, no power. They're empty whether you're talking about something made of stone or a god or goddess you've created in your mind and on paper.

Stop and think for a minute. Would you rather worship and trust something you created, or the One who created you? Something made of wood and gold will not answer or comfort you. Something created by a person's hands with silver and stone cannot know your innermost thoughts.

We were created to trust in God. But people have been rebelling against this idea since the beginning of human history because it means surrendering control of our lives to Him. Solomon, the wisest man who ever lived, described it this way: "Trust in the Lord with all your heart; do not depend on your own understanding. Seek his will in all you do, and he will direct your paths" (Proverbs 3:5–6). God knows what's best for us because He created us (Psalm 139:13–16). If we really want to experience a satisfying and meaningful life, we need to surrender every area of our life over to Him.

God wants us to come to Him with our struggles and doubts. His answers may not be what we expect, but God's going to keep us going by revealing himself to us in various ways. God is the Creator; He is all-powerful. He has a plan and will carry it out if we will trust Him.

God is our strength and place of safety. We can have confidence in God because He is our hope.

Wiccans have bought the same deceptive lie that people living in Egypt did centuries ago. Egypt was a land of many gods, and each one represented a different aspect of life. It was very common to worship a lot of different gods to take care of all your needs and get the maximum benefits. When God told His people who had left Egypt to worship Him, at first they thought He was just one more god to add to the list. But God made it very clear to the Israelites when He said, "Do not worship any other gods besides me" (Exodus 20:3).

Let's think logically for a minute. Why would you want to worship a god that you created? That god would obviously be no greater or more powerful than you, so what help could it possibly be? The God of the Bible is sovereign—supreme, free from external control. He is all-powerful (see Psalm 139:13–16; Jeremiah 32:17; Psalm 115:3). Nothing is too hard for Him. God has the power and ability to see us through any situation in life. The opportunity to create your own deity may sound cool and fascinating, but in the end it's useless and dangerous to your soul.

When it comes to having the freedom to be yourself, the Bible contains a very interesting concept in John 8:32. It says that "you will know the truth, and the truth will set you free." Jesus himself is the source of truth. He does not give us the freedom to do what we want, but to do what God designed for us to do. The truth is that we all need a Savior because of our spiritual disease called sin. Jesus died on a cross to pay the penalty for our sin and set us free to be the people that we were created to be.

Christianity is not about a set of ideas that we buy into; it's about a relationship with a person—Jesus Christ. All other religions—including Wicca—tell us what we need to do. Christianity tells us what God has done for us. And remember, there's nothing you can do to earn this relationship—it's a free gift (Ephesians 2:8).

When we surrender our lives to Jesus, we become brand-new people. Check this out: "What this means is that those who become Christians become new persons. They are not the same anymore, for the old life is gone. A new life has begun!" (2 Corinthians 5:17). We're not rehabilitated or re-educated. We don't just change some stuff; we start a new life under a new Master.

But there's a catch—you have to surrender the old life for the new one. *Surrender* is a dirty word because the world says the way to freedom and becoming an individual is staying in charge.

When it comes to the kingdom of God, things are just the opposite. Jesus said, "If you try to keep your life for yourself, you will lose it. But if you give up your life for me, you will find true life" (Matthew 16:25). Surrendering isn't easy because you give up control. But because you're surrendering to the One who made you and knows what's best for you, you end up gaining a whole lot more than you give up.

WHAT'S IN IT FOR YOU?

So let's say you decide to surrender your life to Jesus; what's in it for you? Before we look at what you'll get, let's get a glimpse of what surrender will cost you.

To start with, basically everything. The Bible says, "God bought you with a high price" (1 Corinthians 6:20). The idea here is one of slaves being purchased at an auction. When Jesus died on the cross, He paid the penalty for our sins and set us free. What Jesus did was the ultimate demonstration of just how much God loves us (Romans 5:8). "This is real love. It is not that we loved God, but that he loved us and sent his Son as a sacrifice to take away our sins" (1 John 4:10). Because of what Jesus did, we are now obligated to serve Him. No place in Wicca will you find that a sacrifice of this significance was ever made by the All or the god and goddess.

Jesus explained the cost of following Him in this way: "If any of you wants to be my follower, you must put aside your selfish ambition, shoulder your cross, and follow me. If you try to keep your life for yourself, you will lose it. But if you give up your life for my sake and for the sake of the Good News, you will find true life" (Mark 8:34–35). The picture here is very vivid: If we want to follow Jesus, we must totally surrender to Him. God wants us to choose to follow Him, to stop trying to control our own destiny and let Him guide us. Once again, this makes good sense. Because God created us and absolutely loves us, He knows what real life is all about. Nothing will satisfy us like an intimate relationship with God.

Because of what God has done for us, He expects us to listen to Him, trust Him, and obey Him. And because of His great love for us, He has set up boundaries to help keep us on the right track and experience life the way He designed for us to. These boundaries, or commandments, are found throughout the Bible. For example, the Ten Commandments are found in Exodus 20. These commands, or guidelines, were meant to help us practically understand God's plan for us and how we should live. And because they come from God, we know they are good for us (Psalm 111:7).

I talk with a lot of people who tell me they used to be Christians, but now they're into Wicca. I think what they're really saying is that they "used to go to church." I'm convinced that people like this never really had a relationship with God or understood what it's all about. If they really knew Jesus, and understood all that He has done for them, they never would have turned to Wicca. So what's it mean to be a follower of Jesus, and what are the benefits?

The first thing that most people think about when it comes to Christianity is going to heaven when they die. Eternal life is definitely one of the benefits when you surrender your life to Jesus (John 6:40). Jesus gives us an incredible promise about heaven in John 14:2–3, "There are many rooms in my Father's home, and I am going to prepare a place for you. If this were not so, I would tell you plainly. When everything is ready, I will come and get you, so that you will always be with me where I am." Jesus is getting everything ready for us, and it's going to be greater than anything we can even imagine (1 Corinthians 2:7–9; Revelation 21:4). God's going to give us new bodies, and we will recognize and be able to spend time with friends and relatives who also trusted Christ (2 Corinthians 5:1; Matthew 17:3–4). What does Wicca offer that even comes close?

Wiccan philosophy embraces the concept of multiple reincarnations. Some Wiccans say that when we die, our soul journeys to a realm variously known as the Land of the Faerie, the Shining Land, and the Land of the Young. This realm is neither heaven nor the underworld.

BUILD YOUR OWN RELIGION — 111

It simply is—a non-physical reality much less dense than ours.[5] Others say our spirit is released back to the place they call Summerland.[6] Either way, they believe the soul needs some "continuing spiritual education," and when the time is right, another carnation of the physical self takes place to go back to earth and continue to work out karma. Each body the soul inhabits on earth is different. No two bodies or lives are the same. This supposedly keeps the soul from getting stagnate. The sex, race, place of birth, economic class, and every other individuality of the soul is determined by its actions in past lives. Wiccan author Scott Cunningham writes, "There's no god or curse or mysterious force of fate upon which we thrust the responsibility for the trials in our lives. We decide what we need to learn in order to evolve, and then it is hoped, during incarnation, work toward this progress. If not, we regress into darkness."[7]

So what happens after the final incarnation? Wiccan teaching is pretty vague on this. But basically after rising up the spiral ladder of life and death and rebirth, Wiccans believe the souls who have attained perfection break away from the reincarnation/karma cycle and merge with the male and female balanced (god and goddess) creator entity.[8] Stop and think. *Reincarnation means that you keep paying for your sins over and over and over again.* After all this time, work, and energy, where is the hope of eternal life? And even more than that, the real you stopped existing somewhere in a past lifetime, so who is it that finally merges with a "force" out in the cosmos somewhere? Doesn't sound real appealing to me.

Stop and think about the spiral of life and death and rebirth in Wicca. Here's a religion that has no absolutes—no right and wrong— no such thing as sin. When someone dies, their soul goes to a holding place to review the past life and see what lessons need to be learned. Then, at the right time, their soul heads back to earth as a different person, maybe even a different sex, to start the process all over again. Basically, because of reincarnation, they get to keep trying to get things

---

[5]Cunningham, 71.
[6]Gary Cantrell, *Wiccan Beliefs and Practices* (St. Paul: Llewellyn Publications, 2003), 27.
[7]Cunningham, 70.
[8]Cantrell, 27.

right—reach perfection, pay for sins—over and over again. Then when their soul finally reaches perfection, you merge with the god and goddess—the All—and cease to exist. Absurd!

When you put the two side by side—Wicca and Christianity—there's no comparison. With Jesus there's no working out or worrying about what happens when you die; God has guaranteed it! (John 10:28). But there's more.

Skeptics usually say, "Big deal, you get a ticket to heaven . . . so what?" There's more to it, a lot more. There's eternal life with the Father. Before I forget, Wiccans don't have a heaven, since most of them believe in reincarnation.

What are some other reasons that would make you want to surrender your life to Jesus—things that affect your life here on earth? Take a look at this list:

- All of your needs will be met (Psalm 34:10; Matthew 6:33)
- Wherever you go, whatever you do, you will be blessed (Deuteronomy 28:1–6)
- Forgiveness (Colossians 1:14)
- Help in times of trouble (Genesis 18:14; Psalm 118:5)
- Meaning in life (John 10:10)
- Adoption into God's family (John 1:12)
- Power to face challenges in life (Philippians 4:13)
- Peace (Philippians 4:7)
- Hope (Psalm 42:5; Hebrews 6:19)
- Direction for life (Psalm 25:8–11)
- Protection (Psalm 18:2–3)
- Purpose in life (Esther 4:13–14; Jeremiah 29:11)
- You are never alone (Hebrews 13:5)
- Joy to rise above your circumstances (John 15:11)
- Unconditional love (John 3:16; 13:27–28)

Take a minute and let what you just read soak in—it's awesome! What can Wicca offer that's even close? But all this is not even close to the benefits that are ours when we know God personally. You'll never experience any of this by standing on the outside looking in. It's like standing outside a candy store and trying to imagine how sweet everything tastes.

IT'S YOUR CHOICE

You'll never survive by trying to "have it your way." Eventually, you're going to get frustrated because things aren't working the way you want. You can try to keep it together on your own, but you'll keep coming up empty-handed. It's your decision and you'll have no one to blame for the outcome except for you. What you decide comes down to how you respond to these three questions:

- Do you trust the Bible?
- Does God exist?
- Who do you say Jesus is?

You have a choice: worship something that you've created, or worship the Savior who created you and understands you better than anyone ever could. He is intimately aware of how you're wired because He put you together. "You made all the delicate, inner parts of my body and knit me together in my mother's womb" (Psalm 139:13).

The God of the Bible is the only one who can satisfy your deepest needs and help you to become the person you were designed to be. But He expects total surrender. Choose wisely—the rest of your life on this planet and all of eternity is on the line.

CHAPTER NINE

GOD, WHERE ARE YOU?

IT WAS THE SUNDAY MORNING AFTER CHRISTMAS when a 9.0 quake jolted the earth and moved trillions of tons of water in Southeast Asia. Silently the water moved outward at the speed of a jet aircraft. As the water approached shore, it began to slow, and large waves were formed. The cataclysmic tsunami crashed onshore, creating unbelievable destruction in its path. The huge wall of water tossed yachts and cars around like they were toys. No one was immune—the devastation and suffering hit lavish vacation resorts and poor fishing villages. Over two hundred thousand people lost their lives, and doctors immediately warned of the possibility of epidemics to come.

After the deadly tsunami hit, people of all faiths were asking, "Why us? Why here? Why now?" You could say this cataclysm was of biblical proportions, but most of the Hindus, Muslims, and Buddhists who were caught up in the disaster and survived had never heard the story of Noah and the God of Wrath.[1] Christians familiar with the Bible were reminded of the story of Job in the Old Testament. He lost everything and was tested to the extreme. But even the account of Job doesn't seem to answer the timeless questions of "Why do bad things happen

---

[1] Kenneth L. Woodward, "Countless Souls Cry Out To God," *Newsweek* magazine, January 10, 2005, 37.

to those who don't deserve it?" and "Why would a loving God allow such suffering?"

According to Ruth Barrett, a Wiccan high priestess who formerly led a group in Los Angeles and now heads a Wisconsin temple dedicated to the Roman goddess Diana, the earthquake and tidal wave were simply a case of "mother nature stretching—she had a kink in her back and stretched." Though the resulting casualties were horrendous, she said, dwelling on why people suffered was narcissistic when nature constantly reshapes itself. "We're so self-centered and think we are the be-all and end-all of the universe," she said.[2] Priestess Barrett doesn't seem to have many answers from her Wiccan beliefs for this tragedy.

What do you think about disasters like the tsunami in Asia? How do you explain what happened? What about suffering in your own life or that of a friend—do you ever feel like shaking your fist in the sky and saying, "God, where are you?"

Wicca embraces those who have turned bitter toward God and those who are disillusioned over not obtaining answers to their prayers or seeing friends and family suffer.

Josh is fifteen years old and says he's a Wiccan. He used to believe in God but doesn't anymore. Wicca suits him much better. He likes being earth-friendly and being able to have a religion that's more comfortable. Besides, if God really cared about him, his mother would still be alive today. But ever since Josh turned his back on God and started practicing Wicca, he still doesn't seem to have a lot of answers about his mom's death and other difficult stuff in his life.

Everyone wonders why a loving God would allow evil to flourish in our world. Wicca answers that question by promising its believers the power to set things right. But in some cases the cost may be higher than what you expect. And where does the power come from?

Two good friends got involved in the craft and decided to pursue another path to find answers about the tough stuff in life. Investigators in Knox, Kentucky, say they may never know what sparked the suicides of Sarah Casey and Debra Kawaguchi. Investigators maintain that the teenage girls deliberately walked together onto railroad tracks and into

---

[2]Teresa Watanabe and Larry B. Stammer, "Deadly Tsunami Resurrects the Old Question of Why," *Los Angeles Times*, Saturday, January 8, 2005, B2.

the path of an oncoming train on Saturday morning, August 28. But the "why" remains unknown.

In an effort to make sense of it all, investigators have been looking into all of the girls' interests. Officials found that they were both interested in Wicca. Detective Oscar Cowen of the Starke County Sheriff's Department said, "The girls may have latched on to some notion of reincarnation and, not understanding what death means, made an ill-informed decision to end their own lives in hopes of returning as better people."[3]

It appears as if no one told Sarah and Debra that suicide is a permanent solution to temporary problems.

How do you handle the pain and suffering of life? There are so many kinds of suffering—abuse, rejection, loneliness, diseases like cancer, physical disabilities, emotional struggles, or the death of a friend or family. Where do you turn for help?

There are answers that I've personally found and experienced. They didn't come easy, but it was worth it.

TOUGH LESSONS

It was a little after 7:00 A.M. when my friends Chuck and Jamie headed west on Highway 58 after traveling up Highway 395. They were part of our ministry team, and they were on their way to central California for some final meetings in preparation for a citywide evangelistic event we were having the following week in Madera. A few minutes later, at approximately seven-thirty that morning, Chuck and Jamie were hit head-on by another vehicle speeding at one hundred miles per hour on the wrong side of the road.

Chuck was killed instantly—the steering wheel of the small truck crushed his chest. The paramedics were able to get Jamie into an ambulance, but he died on the way to the hospital. The four guys in the other car walked away from the accident—they were stone drunk and not injured. I didn't hear about the accident until Chuck's pastor called our office at three o'clock that afternoon. In disbelief I kept telling some

---

[3]Joshua Stowe, "Officials Seek Answers in Teens Deaths," (Indiana: *South Bend Tribune* newspaper—online edition—*www.southbendtribune.com*, September 1, 2004).

of our staff members that the pastor was wrong because Chuck and Jamie were supposed to call me around three-thirty. I was numb and couldn't believe that something this awful could happen.

Over the course of the weeks following the accident I found myself feeling hurt, confused, and angry with God. I'd be crying—which is very unusual for me—then looking up to the sky and yelling, "God—why? Why did Chuck and Jamie have to die?" I reminded God that they were good guys—husbands, fathers—and faithfully serving Him. "What gives, God? How could you let something like this happen?" I wasn't getting anywhere except feeling more and more frustrated. It came down to a choice: I was either going to turn to God to see if He had any answers, or walk away. I decided to dig into the Bible to see if I had missed something. Here are a few of the lessons I learned about pain and suffering after the death of my good friends.

First, God is in control. He is sovereign (Jeremiah 1:6), which means He's free from any external control; He is supreme, excellent, and powerful. We've got to realize that we will never be able to find an explanation for all the things that happen in life. "God has made everything beautiful for its own time. He has planted eternity in the human heart, but even so, people cannot see the whole scope of God's work from beginning to end" (Ecclesiastes 3:11). And we have to learn that God's thoughts are nothing like ours and His ways are beyond what we could even imagine (Isaiah 55:8). We may never know why something has happened; instead, ask God, "What next?" and "How can I best navigate through the troubled waters of my life?"

When you're going through a tough time, do you focus on the circumstances or on God? Our natural tendency is to look for a quick fix, but sometimes God doesn't work as fast as we would like Him to. Don't bail on Him; instead, try to focus on how awesome and powerful He is. The same power that God used to create the heavens and the earth (Genesis 1–2) and to raise Jesus from the dead (Acts 2:32) is available to help you with even the most difficult circumstances in your life.

The next lesson I learned is that pain and suffering are a natural part of life. Living in the United States, we can have a distorted picture about the goodness of God. We tend to think that it means possessing a lot of material stuff and experiencing no problems. And up until 9/

11, most Americans had felt sheltered and protected. It's kind of like, "If we don't do anything real bad, then everything will be fine." But that's not what God says in the Bible. Suffering is an intrusion in God's original design of creation (Genesis 1:31). It's not what He desired. Suffering is a result of sin—trying to live our lives without God. And it all started way back with the first man and woman in the Garden of Eden (Genesis 3:16–19).

Adam and Eve chose to disobey God (sin). They bought the lie from Satan—who was disguised as a serpent. The lie: "You can be god of your own life." People are still being deceived like this today through Wicca. Because God is holy, He had to respond in a way consistent with His perfect moral nature. He had to punish their sin. The consequences of Adam and Eve's sin may seem extreme, but remember their sin set in motion humanity's tendency toward disobeying God. Every person who was ever born—except Jesus—has been born with a sinful nature (Romans 5:12–21), and as a result, pain and suffering became a natural part of life.

God views sin of any kind very seriously. Even in small amounts, sin can prove to be toxic and deadly to our lives. But amazingly, even when we do disobey Him, God is still willing to forgive us. That's something that Wicca doesn't offer.

Jesus promised us that if we followed Him, we would experience pain and suffering. "I have told you all this so that you may have peace in me. Here on earth you will have many trials and sorrows. But take heart, because I have overcome the world" (John 16:33). Jesus wants us to be confident and brave. In spite of the inevitable struggles we will face, He wants us to know that we will never be alone. Jesus does not abandon us in our pain and struggles. He has already won the ultimate victory—over death—when He died on the cross. So we can have His peace even in the toughest times.

And as hard as it may be to understand, God has a purpose in our pain and suffering. Check this out: "Dear brothers and sisters, whenever trouble comes your way, let it be an opportunity for joy. For when your faith is tested, your endurance has a chance to grow" (James 1:2–3). Notice this verse doesn't say *if* trouble comes, but *when* it does. We're going to have troubles, and it's possible to benefit from them. We're not supposed to pretend that we are happy when we are in pain; instead, God wants us to have a positive attitude because of what struggles can produce in our life. We need to turn our times of pain into times of learning. These tough times can teach us perseverance. Once you can get the picture that suffering is part of life, then you can realize the importance of perseverance.

We don't completely understand why God allows evil, but we do know that He is able to bring glory to himself through evil by expressing the grace (God's unmerited favor and goodness) and justice that are part of His character. Check out what the Bible says in Romans 9:22–23: "God has every right to exercise his judgment and his power, but he also has the right to be very patient with those who are the objects of his judgment and are fit only for destruction. He also has the right to pour out the riches of his glory upon those he prepared to be the objects of his mercy—even upon us, whom he selected." God is free to act however He chooses because He's God. This includes dealing in patience and mercy with those who have used the freedom of choice to do evil rather than to follow Him. But even though God hates sin and must ultimately judge it, His goodness and love will always overcome.

By allowing evil and wickedness—and the freedom to choose—into our world, God can demonstrate His awesome love and care for each one of us.

Seventeen-year-old Chris called *Life on the Edge—Live!* one Saturday night. He was having problems with how unfair life seems to be. He talked about the tsunami in Asia; friends and relatives dying too soon; people who wanted to be parents that couldn't have children, while those who didn't want children had them. He brought up the issue of money and why some people have a lot of it and others have nothing. Susie Shellenberger (my co-host) and I tried to help him understand that life isn't fair. But that doesn't mean God has abandoned us; instead, He wants to turn our hardships into opportunities for growth.

As hard as it is to do, we need to look at life from God's perspective: eternally. We live in a sinful world and things will never be totally fair in this life, but eventually there will be justice—in God's way and in His time. Fairness is based on human effort, while justice is impartial.

Ideal fairness can only be accomplished by God.

You may not be experiencing pain in your life right now, but eventually you will—then what? How will you cope?

Finally, when we're facing difficult times, we need to trust in God and His character. In what I've experienced, I've realized that it's one thing to stand in front of an audience or talk about this subject on the radio, but it's much different when you are clinging to God's promises yourself because of the pain you're going through. I can tell you from personal experience that God is faithful even in the darkest times. God is powerful and completely loving, not a cowering genie in a bottle—a mystical, impersonal force out in the cosmos somewhere.

From generation to generation God has revealed himself as a personal God who wants an intimate relationship with His people. He wants us to see Him, know Him, speak with Him, and ultimately trust Him. And when we do trust Him, God promises to help us. "Do not be afraid or discouraged, for the LORD is the one who goes before you. He will be with you; he will neither fail you nor forsake you" (Deuteronomy 31:8). Check out this promise in Job: "But by means of their suffering, he rescues those who suffer. For he gets their attention through adversity" (36:15).

Sometimes God uses pain and suffering as a form of discipline we need to get back on the right track (Psalm 119:67, 71, 75; Hebrews 12:6–10; 1 Corinthians 11:31–32). Most of the time He uses it to help us grow stronger and build character in our lives (Proverbs 25:4). God wants us to become better, not bitter, about the circumstances in our lives. And don't forget, He always does what is best for us. "And we know that God causes everything to work together for the good of those who love God and are called according to his purpose" (Romans 8:28). This verse doesn't mean that everything that happens to us is good, because there is evil in the world. But God does work for our good in everything—every situation—not just in isolated situations. And remember, because He is God He sees the big picture of our life— beginning to end.

The best way to practically apply these lessons is through prayer. Wiccans would call it using the cone of power. Take Wayne, a high school student who sent me the following e-mail:

"The cone of power is no different than Christian prayer. You ask God for help to cure your cancer-stricken mother; you focus your mind to attain this end. You want it with your whole body and soul because you love her and want her to be well. What is so wrong with that? Because people do not pray to your specific God, are they wrong and going to an eternal damnation? If that is what your 'loving God' is like, I want nothing to do with Him."

In actuality, the cone of power is *very* different from prayer. The cone of power is a method of directing the energy of an individual or group for a singular purpose or to provide a connection to spirit. This energy is a combination of love, creativity, and spirit, and forms the basis for a witch's power, which he or she raises to accomplish a desire. A witch builds up energy by chanting and swaying. Once the heat from the energy has reached a certain level, it must be directed into a magickal tool or objective, where it can be held. At the desired time the energy can be sent out to achieve the desired result.

When Christians pray, we are asking God for help because we recognize that we have no power or ability in ourselves to affect a change in a situation or help someone. It is not a matter of focusing our mind on a particular end, but rather demonstrating our total dependence upon God to act, according to His will. The God of the Bible is a God of love and wants the best for each one of us, and that includes securing our eternal destiny in heaven. He made this possible through Jesus' death on the cross.

Prayer in its simplest form is having a conversation with God— talking to Him, then quietly listening and waiting for His answer. In all the years that I've been following Jesus, I've never heard an audible voice from the sky. But my prayers have been answered in a variety of ways—including "No." That's the hard part—trusting that God loves me so much that He will always do what is best for me in every situation—if I depend on Him. That's where faith comes in. "Faith . . . is the confident assurance that what we hope for is going to happen. It is the evidence of things we cannot yet see" (Hebrews 11:1). The beginning point of faith is believing in God's character: that He is who He says.

But the Bible teaches that God has only committed himself to answer the prayers of His children. "The eyes of the Lord watch over those who do right, and his ears are open to their prayers. But the Lord turns his face against those who do evil" (1 Peter 3:12). That could be one reason why you have not experienced answers to your prayers—you have not put your faith and trust in Jesus. God has chosen to do nothing for us until we let Him do something in us.

If you have not surrendered your life to Christ, then the next chapter, "Whose Word You Gonna Trust?", is for you. Pay careful attention to what you read.

A PARTNER FOR LIFE

There is help and hope in the midst of pain and suffering—it's found in the person of Jesus. "Come to me, all of you who are weary and carry heavy burdens, and I will give you rest. Take my yoke upon you. Let me teach you, because I am humble and gentle, and you will find rest for your souls. For my yoke is easy to bear, and the burden I give you is light" (Matthew 11:28–30).

A yoke is a heavy wooden harness that fits over the shoulders of an ox or oxen, and it's attached to a piece of equipment that the ox or oxen pull. Are you pulling a heavy load around? It could be any number of things—bad health, being a victim of bullying, a broken home, rejection, unconfessed sin, or even weariness in your search for God. Jesus can free you from these burdens. The rest He promises is love, healing, and peace with God. But it doesn't mean the end of problems or hard work. The difference is that with Jesus we don't face the difficulties alone, because now the weight of our pain falls on His shoulders, which are much bigger than ours.

Whatever pain and suffering you are facing, don't go through it alone. Put aside your misconceptions about God and let Him take over. Make Jesus your first resource rather than your last resort. It won't be easy, but it will be worth it. When pain and suffering hit your life, and doubts begin to flood your mind and heart, put your confidence in God and don't give up!

WHOSE WORD YOU GONNA TRUST?

WHEN IT COMES TO ADVICE ABOUT one of the fastest-growing religions in North America, there's plenty of it to go around. Go online and you'll find thousands of Web sites about Wicca and the craft. Walk into a bookstore and you'll find dozens of books—like *The Teen Spell Book* and *The Complete Idiot's Guide to Wicca and Witchcraft*—by people like Gary Cantrell, Phyllis Curott, Jamie Wood, and even celebrities like Fiona Horne.

There are some people who call Silver Ravenwolf—Wiccan priestess and director of the International Wiccan/Pagan Press Alliance—"Mama Silver" because "she cares so much about those who read her books."[1] Her writing covers everything from spells for homework and dating to all anyone needs to know to become a pentacle-wearing, spell-casting authentic witch.

Scott Cunningham is the author of more than thirty books on Wicca, including one of the most widely recommended Wiccan books, *A Guide for the Solitary Practitioner*. Cunningham tells his readers that

[1]Silver Ravenwolf, *Teen Witch* (St. Paul: Llewellyn Publications, 2000), xv.

Wicca is varied and multi-faceted, and as in every religion, the Wiccan experience is one shared with deity alone. "I write based on my experiences and the instruction I have received to practice Wicca."[2]

Wiccan psychic Michele Morgan wants to help her readers make simple what she calls a complex religion, science, art, and way of life. "It is my desire to simplify what can seem positively overwhelming by taking you out of the 'head' and into the 'heart' of the Wiccan way. If you experience something first, it can be far easier to assimilate the myriad details that go into creating it."[3]

They want to seem like sincere people who mean well and want to help others find a way to make sense out of life. But where are the facts? Everything they write is based on feelings and experiences, which are obviously both elements of spirituality. But there's more to it. Do you really want to base the rest of your life and your eternal destiny on someone's feelings and experiences? There's too much at stake to be that careless and haphazard.

In this chapter I want to challenge you to set aside your prejudices—things you've heard from friends, teachers, relatives, and even some things you may have read about God, Jesus, and the Bible. I want you to think. See if you can connect the "dots" of information. I want you to evaluate what you are about to read. Try to answer the following questions for yourself:

• Can I trust the Bible?
• Does God really exist? And what is He like?
• Who is Jesus?

The next few pages could be the most important ones you ever read. I believe that the answers you've been looking for about spirituality are here. Be open and think.

THE BIBLE

Skylar's been struggling with understanding where the Bible came from, especially in trying to explain it to her friends at school. Over and

---

[2]Scott Cunningham, *Wicca: A Guide for the Solitary Practitioner* (St. Paul: Llewellyn Publications, 2003), xi-xii.
[3]Michele Morgan, *Simple Wicca*, (Berkeley: Conari Press, 2000), xi.

over again the question keeps coming up: "How do we know that someone didn't just make up the Bible?"

The Bible is not a collection of stories, myths, fables, or simple human ideas about God. It's not a human book.

In 2 Timothy 3:16 we read that "all Scripture is inspired by God and is useful to teach us what is true and to make us realize what is wrong in our lives. It straightens us out and teaches us to do what is right." In other words, the Bible is literally God-breathed. Inspiration is the mysterious, unprecedented process by which God breathed His truth into and through human writers. Those writers wrote out of their own historical and cultural contexts, and even though they used their individual minds and unique abilities, they wrote what God wanted them to write.

But be careful in how you use and understand the term *inspiration*. Usually we think of a singer, author, or artist being "inspired" in their work, which means we think it's really good. But when this same word is applied to the Bible, it has a different meaning. The Bible has been "breathed" by God. The Bible claims to be His very Word; it has come from His very mouth.[4] No other religious book has ever made this claim, nor is it as historically reliable as the Bible. The authors of the Bible—most of them prophets—spoke God's words. A prophet was someone who was supposed to say exactly what God told him to say (Jeremiah 26:2; Exodus 4:30). God didn't verbally dictate the Bible to each author, yet the end result is just as precise as if He had. God supernaturally supervised what they wrote, and because God was in control of its writing, the Bible is completely trustworthy.

The Bible is the most unique book ever written. It's the written Word of God. The Bible was written over a fifteen-hundred-year span of time by forty-four different authors—all living in different places—in three different languages (Hebrew, Aramaic, and Greek)—on three different continents (Asia, Africa, and Europe). It's an amazing book in its unity in the middle of its vast diversity. Think about it. The Bible has one continuous drama from Genesis to Revelation—the rescue of humanity. It has a central theme—the person of Jesus Christ. And from

[4]Josh McDowell, *The New Evidence That Demands a Verdict* (Nashville: Thomas Nelson, 1999), 334.

the beginning to the end, the Bible has one unified message: Humanity's problem is sin and the remedy is found in Jesus. All this evidence points to the idea that there was one mind behind the writing of the Bible—God's.

The Bible's internal claims to inspiration and divine authority eliminate the possibility of it being "a remarkable collection of literature" or "an oft-reliable handbook of principles and ethics." Since nothing that claims to be from God and *isn't* from God can be in any sense trustworthy, Scripture (like Jesus) demands a verdict—true or false.

The uniqueness of the Bible's message can be summed up in Romans 6:23. "For the wages of sin is death, but the free gift of God is eternal life through Christ Jesus our Lord." Christianity teaches that all people are spiritually dead, and there is no hope for the possibility that we can fix ourselves. Other religions say just the opposite. They agree there is something wrong spiritually, but they hold out hope that somehow, through some kind of human effort, we can be fixed. The Bible makes it clear that spiritually dead people can't fix themselves (Ephesians 2:8–9). And because God is holy, He cannot have a relationship with sinful people. The problem is that we all have sinned (Romans 3:23).

But even though we have this horrible spiritual condition, there is good news—God has a remedy. We can have eternal life—not just some continued existence on another spiritual plane after death; we can actually have fellowship with God himself (John 17:3). No other religion in the world promises us eternal life and closeness with the living God (Hebrews 4:16). And it starts in this life—the moment we place our faith and trust in Jesus Christ. Finally, this message is unique because eternal life is a free gift. It's not a gift that can be earned; it can only be received. We can have this gift by admitting our need for life because of our spiritual death—and then relying on the work that Jesus did for us by paying the penalty for our sin.

No other book ever written has had the kind of circulation the Bible has had. Billions of copies have been sold and distributed around the world. According to the United Bible Societies, the Bible, and portions of it, has now been translated into more than twenty-two hundred languages.

The Bible is also unique in its ability to have survived over the course of time, through countless attempts at destruction and persecution. It actually has more ancient manuscript evidence to support it than any ten pieces of classical literature combined.[5] Throughout history people have tried to burn and outlaw the Bible. Others have spent their lives trying to refute it—even so-called scholars. Yet the Bible has endured all its enemies and has been able to stand up to even the most persistent critics.

When tested by the same criteria by which other historical manuscripts are tested, the Bible demonstrates incredible accuracy for the historical events it reports. For example, did you know that there are 5,656 partial and complete manuscript portions (in Greek) of just the New Testament alone? In comparison, the next closest historical manuscript is Homer's *Iliad*, with only 643 copies. Then we need to consider supporting evidence that comes from sources like early Christian writers outside the Bible like Clement of Rome, Ignatius, or Polycarp. Or consider support from non-Christian historical writers like Tacitus and Josephus.

Or how about the incredible statements about the earth, the heavens, and the body the Bible makes that pre-date their discoveries by anywhere from two thousand to three thousand years—things like deep valleys and huge mountains (2 Samuel 22:16; Job 38:16; Jonah 2:6), or the concept of allowing the ground to remain unplowed and unused every seventh year (Exodus 23:10–11), which is accurate information but was way ahead of its time.

In the 1840s pregnant women had a one-in-six rate of dying from "childbirth fever" if they went to a particular hospital in Vienna, Austria. Dr. Ignaz Semmelweis noticed something in common about their deaths. Doctors who had just completed an autopsy on victims of "childbirth fever" had examined all the women who died. So Dr. Semmelweis implemented a new policy that all doctors must wash their hands after performing an autopsy. As a result, the death rate among pregnant women dropped radically to one in eighty-four. What's significant about this story is that God set down cleanliness laws through

---

[5]Ibid., 9.

Moses thirty-five hundred years before Dr. Semmelweis's policy on doctors' washing their hands (Numbers 19:17, 19).

We must also examine archaeological evidence that supports the Bible. Well-known archaeologist Nelson Glueck said, "It may be stated categorically that no archaeological discovery has ever controverted a biblical reference. Scores of archaeological findings have been made which conform in clear outline or exact detail historical statements in the Bible."[6] There can be no question as to the historical reliability of the Bible.

The Bible is unique because it is the only book in the world ever written to offer specific predictions about the future hundreds of years in advance that were literally fulfilled. A lot of these predictions focus on the first and second coming of Christ. There are several unique things about prophecies in the Bible in contrast to other attempts made to predict the future events. These unique features include:

- The prophecies were very specific.
- None of these predictions ever failed.
- Since the prophecies about Christ were written hundreds of years before His birth, no one could have even been making intelligent guesses.
- Many of these predictions were beyond human ability to somehow force fulfillment.

The best way to explain how all this was possible is the existence of a living God who knows all things—the beginning from the end (Isaiah 46:10).

When you hear some psychic on TV or read their predictions in a newspaper or magazine, remember a very important test for false prophets—whether their predictions came to pass (Deuteronomy 18:22). In biblical times, those whose predictions failed were stoned to death (Deuteronomy 18:20). If that happened today, it would cause some serious hesitation on the part of some people—maybe even cause them to find another line of work! Biblical prophets were not known to have made even one error in the course of hundreds of predictions.

---

[6]Dean C. Halverson, *The Compact Guide to World Religions* (Minneapolis: Bethany House Publishers, 1996), 256.

Another sure way of distinguishing true prophets from false ones is by miracles (Acts 2:22; Hebrews 2:3–4). Miracles are confirmation that a prophet is actually speaking for God because they are supernatural acts of God. And if you examine all the other religious leaders in the world, you will find that only the Judeo-Christian leaders were supernaturally confirmed by genuine miracles that couldn't possibly be some form of mental or emotional experience or some kind of trickery. Moses, Elijah, Paul, and Peter performed miraculous signs among the people (Exodus 4:1; 1 Kings 18; Acts 2:4, 3:1–10, 20:10). But more importantly, the ministry of Jesus was marked and accredited by God through miracles, signs, and wonders (Acts 2:22).

We could talk about the Bible's unique impact on civilization, as well as on literature. But we must also recognize its unique teachings on character, history, and prophecy. It's amazing when you consider all the future events throughout history that have occurred which were predicted in the Bible hundreds, sometimes even thousands, of years in advance. No unconditional prophecy of the Bible about events to the present day has gone unfilled. Other books claim divine inspiration, such as the Koran, the Book of Mormon, and parts of the (Hindu) Veda. But none of those books contains predictive prophecy that is completely accurate.[7] Hundreds of predictions—at times given hundreds of years in advance—have been literally fulfilled. Fulfilled prophecy is another glaring sign of the unique divine authority of the Bible.

The Bible is our ultimate source of truth. It doesn't make any sense why anyone would want to base his or her eternal destiny—and life on the planet—purely on someone's opinions, feelings, or experiences when we have God's Word—the Bible—available to help us and guide us. The core message of the Bible, which sets it apart from any other book in all of history, is the offer of the free gift of eternal life through Jesus Christ.

Use the Bible as God intended—as an immovable anchor for your life.

---

[7]Ibid., 12.

GOD

Bruce Almighty, a movie starring Jim Carrey, is a story about a local TV news reporter who is discontented with nearly everything in his life, and he rarely misses an opportunity to complain about it. After being fired from his job and having the worst day of his life, Bruce rages and rails against the Lord for his rotten luck. He then experiences a series of curious signs, which eventually lead him to an old building where he meets a nondescript janitor (Morgan Freeman) who ultimately reveals that he is God. He's heard Bruce's complaints and now has an offer for the choleric newscaster—His job!

God gives Bruce all His powers and challenges him to take on the big job to see if he can do any better. Bruce proceeds to utilize these infinite powers for his own amusement, advancement, and advantage until he finally stands at a crossroads. He must decide whether or not he will become the biggest jerk in the universe or find a little bit of humanity in "Bruce Almighty."

Once again Hollywood has given us an interesting look at God and what He might be like. Curious as it may be to think about God giving away His power, it's far from the truth and nowhere close to reality. So what about God—does He really exist? And if He does, what's He like?

There are those in Wicca who teach that it's ultimately up to each person to decide whether the Divine is one great power or many. They also say that it's a personal thing as to what characteristics of the god, goddess, or other deities witches look to for guidance and support in their daily spiritual journey. We talked a lot about this earlier in chapter 8, "Build Your Own Religion."

So how do we know that God exists? Are there valid reasons for believing, or are we supposed to accept Him by blind faith?

Your entire life on earth and after death is affected by whether you see yourself as god of your life or if you acknowledge and submit to the living God—one who is to be respected and loved.

What evidence is there for God? To begin with, you can't examine Him in a test tube or prove Him with usual scientific methodology. However, we can say with equal emphasis that it's not possible, by scientific method, to prove that the French general Napoleon ever lived. The reason lies in the nature of history itself and in the limitations of the scientific method.[8] In order for something to be proved scientifically, it must be repeatable. History is not repeatable. That something or someone cannot be repeated does not disprove their reality, so it's irrational to suggest that somehow the reality of God can or should be proved scientifically.

Those who work in the field of anthropology have indicated that there is a universal belief in God among the most remote peoples of the globe today. In the earliest histories and legends of peoples all around the world, the original concept was that of one God, who is Creator. An original high God appears to have been in their consciousness even in those societies that are today polytheistic.[9] It is increasingly clear that the oldest traditions everywhere were of one supreme God.[10]

Brilliant men throughout history have concluded this very thing. Augustine said, "Our hearts are restless until they can rest in thee." The great seventeenth-century mathematician, Blaise Pascal, talked about the "God-shaped vacuum" in the heart of each person. Centuries ago Solomon, thought to be the wisest man to ever live, wrote these words: "God has made everything beautiful for its own time. He has planted eternity in the human heart, but even so, people cannot see the whole scope of God's work from beginning to end" (Ecclesiastes 3:11).

It's the law of cause and effect. There's graffiti on the walls at school; someone painted it—the stuff didn't just appear. There's a tree in your front yard—it must have been planted there. Nothing comes from nothing. From the beginning of human existence, we as people—our beings—have had to have a cause. So do this planet and the rest of the universe. *The cause is God.* Where, then, did God originate? He didn't. God is eternal . . . self-existent . . . uncreated. Everything else that lives has life because God *is*.

Look at it another way. The computer that I used to write this book could not have been made without an intelligent designer; it was never going to combine and appear by random chance. Or how about something else even more complex—our bodies. Stop reading right now and

---

[8]Paul E. Little, *Know Why You Believe* (Downers Grove, IL: InterVarsity Press, 2000), 23.
[9]Ibid.
[10]Samuel Zwemer, *The Origin of Religion* (Neptune, N.J.: Loizeaux Bros., 1945), n.p.

go look in a mirror. Think logically: We couldn't possibly have evolved from a single cell in the bottom of a streambed somewhere to eventually become this incredibly fine-tuned, intricate organism that we are without an intelligent designer or creator.

Or what about the design and order of the universe? Think about the planets and the stars—about their placement in the heavens, their function, and the position of the earth. If the earth were any closer to the sun, we'd all be crispy critters. If we were any farther away, we'd all be blocks of ice. Or how about gravity? Everything in life screams out that someone must have put everything together and is maintaining it.

Consider another piece of evidence for God's existence. C. S. Lewis talks about "right and wrong being a clue to the meaning of the universe." Inside of each one of us is a command or influence trying to get us to behave in a certain way.[11] People basically appeal to some sense of right and wrong. For example, I have received a lot of e-mails from Wiccans wanting to know why Christians just can't accept the Wiccan religion. Something inside of them is triggering this desire to be accepted and do what's right. You can see this in a variety of ways in even the smallest activities of life. It comes down to a sense of what ought to take place. It's more than just cultural norms; it's morals. So if there is a moral law inside of each of us, there must be a moral lawgiver. The Bible says that we are made in God's image, setting us apart from all other creation. No other part of creation will ever discuss what is right or wrong. Ever hear this coming from a tree, a rock, or how about a dog or cat? There is somebody behind the universe. He is God—who has a mind, emotions, conscience, and will—a complete personality.[12] "They demonstrate that God's law is written within them, for their own consciences either accuse them or tell them they are doing what is right" (Romans 2:15).

One final piece of evidence to consider is God's presence in the changed lives of people. When someone puts his or her faith and trust in Jesus Christ, there is an incredible change that takes place in an individual's life. Think about stories you have heard about people going

[11]Little, 32.
[12]Ibid., 33.

through unbelievable tragedy or trials in life and God has given them strength, peace, and hope. Why are people all over the globe today giving up everything to follow Jesus?

Each one of us must decide: Do we believe that the human race and the universe just happened, or is it the result of divine design by an all-knowing and all-powerful God?

The Bible never makes an effort to prove that God exists; it assumes that He always has. The terms used to describe what God is like are called attributes. When you begin to grasp these descriptive characteristics of God, you will see another reason why Christianity is so unique compared to other religions in the world. So what is God really like?

- God is all-powerful (omnipotent). It is His power that created the earth and everything in it (Job 42:2; Psalm 115:3; Jeremiah 32:17; Mathew 19:26).

- God is all-knowing (omniscient). He is familiar with all our thoughts and actions and has the answers to the issues of life (Psalm 139:1–6; Isaiah 46:9–10; John 2:25).

- God is changeless (immutable). God is not subject to changes in society or culture; He always remains the same (Psalm 102:27; Hebrews 13:8; James 1:17).

- God is perfection (holiness). God has no equal in holiness; He alone is the standard of ethical purity (Exodus 15:11; Psalm 24:3; Isaiah 40:25; Habakkuk 1:13).

- God is timeless (eternal). He has no beginning and no end. There's never been a time when He has not existed (Deuteronomy 33:27; Isaiah 44:6, 57:15; John 5:26).

- God is unlimited (infinite). He is not confined by the universe or time-space boundaries (1 Kings 8:27; 2 Chronicles 2:6; Psalm 147:5; Jeremiah 23:24; Acts 17:24–28).

- God is separate from His creation (transcendent—above and beyond). He is the source of all life and is self-existing (Isaiah 57:15).

- God is also present in His creation (immanent—near to) (Isaiah 57:15).

- God is in all places at all times (omnipresent). He is completely present everywhere. God is with you no matter where you go. There is no place where God cannot be found (Psalm 139:7–12; Jeremiah 23:23–24).

- God is spirit. He is not composed of matter and does not possess a physical nature. Even though He is a spirit—without a physical body—God is still very real (Psalm 145:13; John 1:18, 4:24; 1 Timothy 1:17, 6:15–16).

- God is personal. He is an individual being, with self-consciousness and will, capable of feeling, choosing, and having a reciprocal relationship with other personal and social beings.[13] We can learn more about God's personality in the Bible. Begin with the fact that God has a name. In Exodus 3:14, He identifies himself as "I AM." This shows us that He is not just some nameless force floating around in the universe. Another sign of God's personal nature is His activity, especially knowing and interacting with people—humans. This developed early in His relationship with humankind—regular talks with Adam and Eve in Genesis 3. He has all the capabilities associated with personality: knowing, feeling, willing, and acting. God sees, hears, speaks, and remembers (Numbers 11:1; 2 Timothy 2:19).

- God is love (all-loving). His love is perfect because it is divine. God's love can be seen throughout the Bible, beginning to end. This is the very nature of God. God's love is a rational and voluntary affection, not just some emotional impulse. Ultimately, "God is love" was expressed through Jesus in His three years of ministry, peaking with

---

[13]Millard J. Erickson, *Christian Theology*, 2nd ed. (Grand Rapids, MI: Baker Books, 1998), 295.

His death on the cross. "For God so loved the world that he gave his only Son, so that everyone who believes in him will not perish but have eternal life" (John 3:16). (See also Hosea 11:4; Jeremiah 31:3; Mark 1:41, 10:16; Luke 15:1; 1 John 4:8, 10.)

- God is truth. By definition truth means that the facts conform to reality; truth identifies things as they are.[14] He is the one true God distinct from all others; there is no other like Him. His Word—the Bible—is reliable and therefore He can be trusted. God is the source of all truth, the beginning of all knowledge, and He makes it available to us so we can have a relationship with Him. (See Isaiah 44:8–10, 45:5; Numbers 23:19; Romans 3:3–4; John 14:1, 2, 6; Hebrews 6:18; Titus 1:2.)

You've just read a lot of biblical support for belief in God. And based on what you read earlier in this chapter, you know that the Bible is more reliable than any book ever written. But the Bible does not support some kind of leap-in-the-dark faith. Biblical faith is based on facts. God is not some vague All, or force, or some imaginary thought. Instead, God is someone who loves us more than we can comprehend and who has made himself known to us.

Go back and re-read the section in this chapter on the Bible. Pay careful attention to the evidence and support for the Bible in prophecy, science, history, and archaeology. This is not only evidence for the Bible but for God as well. All of this didn't just happen by accident and somehow fall into place. It is because of the existence of a living, all-knowing, all-powerful God.

Ultimately, one of the most incredible arguments for the existence of God is when He became a man in the person of Jesus Christ. The world was given all the proof necessary through fulfilled prophecy and the Resurrection.

JESUS CHRIST

Jesus is absolutely essential to Christianity. Without Him, Christianity has no substance or life. Muhammed isn't vital to the philosophy of

---

[14]Ibid., 192.

Islam, nor is Buddha to Buddhism, but the person of Jesus Christ and His work determines everything about Christianity.

- Jesus had a virgin birth. The Bible, in Matthew and Luke, makes it clear that the Holy Spirit conceived Christ (Matthew 1:18; Luke 1:35). Mary had no involvement with a man prior to the birth of Jesus (Matthew 1:18–25).

- The man Jesus was fully God. He was not a man becoming God, but rather God coming into human flesh from the outside (John 1:1, 1:14, 10:30; Titus 2:13; 1 John 5:20).

- Jesus was also fully man. Because He was fully man, He can completely understand and empathize with us (Hebrews 2:16–18; Matthew 1:18, 4:2, 9:36; Luke 2:40; John 4:6, 8:40, 11:35, 19:28).

- Jesus claimed the authority of God. He said He had the power to forgive sins, raise the dead, and would come in the clouds and sit at the right hand of the Father (Mark 2:10, 14:62; John 6:39–40, 10:17–18).

- Jesus had the attributes of God. These qualities were openly displayed in Jesus for everyone to see and experience (Matthew 28:18, 20; Mark 3:10, 4:39; Luke 4:35; John 2:7–11, 25; Ephesians 1:19–21).

- Jesus is the Creator and the Sustainer. He is the divine designer and the one who keeps everything in the universe (John 1:3; Hebrews 1:3; Colossians 2:9).

- Jesus is timeless and eternal. He had no beginning and has no end. Jesus has always been the Son of God at some point in time (John 8:57–58).

- Jesus is the second person of the Trinity (the Son) revealed through flesh (John 1:1; Colossians 1:15–19; 1 John 5:7–8).

• Jesus is truth. He does not just tell the truth, He is the measure, the principle, and the standard for all truth (John 1:17, 14:6, 18:37).

The bottom line when you are examining any religion or belief system is to find out what they believe about Jesus. If it is anything less than what we have outlined above, you know that you are not dealing with the truth. "This is the way to find out if they have the Spirit of God: If a prophet acknowledges that Jesus Christ became a human being, that person has the Spirit of God. If a prophet does not acknowledge Jesus, that person is not from God. Such a person has the spirit of the Antichrist. You have heard that he is going to come into the world, and he is already here" (1 John 4:2–3).

THE DEATH OF JESUS

Jesus died for humanity's sin (the Atonement). Christ died in our place—He was our substitute—purchasing our freedom, making peace with God on our behalf, and satisfying the righteous demands of a holy God. His death is also called vicarious, which means "one in place of another." Isaiah 53:5 puts it this way: "But he was pierced for our transgressions, he was crushed for our iniquities" (NIV).

Because Jesus became human, He was mortal and could actually die for our sins. The death that Jesus suffered was not only humiliating, it was designed to be a death by torture.

But because He was without sin, He was the perfect sacrificial offering for our sin. Jesus was the perfect mediator between the holy God and sinful people (Mark 10:45; Romans 3:25, 5:6–8; Colossians 1:20; 1 Timothy 2:5; 1 Peter 3:18, 2:24; Hebrews 4:15).

The death of Jesus Christ on the cross points out the uniqueness of Christianity. God did for us what we could not do for ourselves. He provided a way in which our sins could be forgiven and we could be brought into an intimate relationship with our Father in heaven. In other words, God made the first move. This is exactly opposite of what needs to happen in pagan religions. We do not make peace with God; it is God who makes peace with us. It isn't God who is brought back together with us, we are reunited to Him.

Wicca operates on a "do it for yourself" plan. Only Christianity

offers salvation as a free gift, and this comes as a result of the unbelievable love God demonstrated for us when Jesus died on a cross to pay
the penalty for our sins. Jesus' death provided redemption for us. The
Bible teaches that we "were bought at a price" (1 Corinthians 6:20 NIV).
The idea pictured here is that of a slave being purchased in a public
slave market. Jesus has purchased us out of the slave market of sin and
has set us free (1 Corinthians 7:23; Galatians 3:13).

Keep in mind that we know more about the details of the death of
Jesus than we know about the death of any other one man in the entire
ancient world.[15]

THE RESURRECTION

Without the Resurrection, everything else about Christianity
becomes meaningless, including the death of Christ. Romans 4:25
reminds us that Jesus was "delivered over to death for our sins and was
raised to life for our justification" (NIV). In His death He took on all
our sins, made us right with God, and in His resurrection He guaranteed us a place in heaven. The empty tomb assures us that all the things
Jesus taught were true.

To fully grasp the importance of the Resurrection, it would be good
for us to clearly define it. The Resurrection mentioned in the Bible is
physical, not spiritual. In the original language of the New Testament
Greek, the word used for *resurrection* is *anastasis nekrôn*. This literally
means the "standing up of a corpse." Thus, *resurrection* in the Bible
means "to stand up," and it always refers to the body. Author and
Oxford scholar C. S. Lewis used to debate with the liberals of his day
in England regarding their position that the Resurrection was only spiritual. Lewis would ask, "What position does a spirit take when it stands
up?"

Just think about the promise that is ours as Christians. One day our
dead bodies are going to "stand up" from the grave! When Paul writes
about the Resurrection in 1 Corinthians 15, he is not talking about a
spiritual resurrection, because the soul never dies. The moment a body
dies, the soul goes somewhere. According to 2 Corinthians 5:6–8, the

---

[15]McDowell, 211.

minute a child of God is absent from the body, he is in the presence of the Lord. The fantastic thing about the Christian faith is that we never view death as the end. Instead, we look into eternity and see the hope that is offered through the resurrected life of Jesus Christ.

Let's look more closely at 1 Corinthians 15:3–8, where Paul writes about the proof of the Resurrection and its prominence in the Gospel.

> "I passed on to you what was most important and what had also been passed on to me—that Christ died for our sins, just as the Scriptures said. He was buried, and he was raised from the dead on the third day, as the Scriptures said. He was seen by Peter and then by the twelve apostles. After that, he was seen by more than five hundred of his followers at one time, most of whom are still alive, though some have died by now. Then he was seen by James and later by all the apostles. Last of all, I saw him, too, long after the others, as though I had been born at the wrong time."

Paul says that he's a communicator of the gospel. The gospel—"good news"—contains three essential facts: Jesus died for you and me, He was buried, and He rose again. There is no gospel apart from these facts. Notice there is nothing that we must do. Rather, it tells us what Jesus has already done for us. It's great news that Christ died and rose again, that He didn't just vanish. His tomb is empty and He is alive today. This gospel is not only great news, but it also has the power to change lives.

A few verses later in 1 Corinthians 15, Paul puts down a series of "ifs" as a demonstration of the importance of the resurrection of Jesus Christ. There was no question in Paul's mind that Christ might not have raised from the dead. Let's examine these "ifs" in light of the importance of the Resurrection.

1. "For if there is no resurrection of the dead, then Christ has not been raised either" (v. 13). The resurrection of the dead and Christ's rising are linked together. Based on His resurrection, Christ is the first and there will be more to follow—those who have placed their faith and trust in Him.

2. "And if Christ was not raised, then all our preaching is useless, and your trust in God is useless" (v. 14). Not only is it a waste of time

to talk about Jesus, but so is Christianity a waste if Jesus has not risen from the dead physically. You might as well stop going to church and reading your Bible. There's no reason to do any of this if Christ had not conquered death.

3. "And we apostles would all be lying about God, for we have said that God raised Christ from the grave, but that can't be true if there is no resurrection of the dead" (v. 15). People don't die for what they know is a lie. But there've been many individuals—including teenagers—who've died for a lie when they thought it was the truth. Just think of the tens of thousands of terrorists who have died for a "cause" because they believed in their leaders. The apostles were so certain that they had seen Jesus after He came back from the grave that they were willing to die for that truth.

4. "If there is no resurrection of the dead, then Christ has not been raised. And if Christ has not been raised, then your faith is useless and you are still under condemnation of your sins. In that case, all who have died believing in Christ have perished!" (v. 16–18). If Jesus hasn't conquered death, then we're all in big trouble. It means that we're all headed for an eternity in hell without Jesus. There's no hope of eternal life. Think of the millions upon millions of people throughout history who've died trusting Christ as their Savior. If Jesus is not alive, then every single one of them has perished.

5. "And if we have hope in Christ only for this life, we are the most miserable people in the world" (v. 19). Christianity is not just a religion for this life; it's a relationship for eternity. If Jesus has not conquered death, then we've been deceived and are the most miserable people on the planet. Instead, we celebrate because we know that Jesus is alive!

The evidence that Jesus actually died and rose from the grave confirms His uniqueness and proves that He is the Son of God. No one else in history has ever been able to predict His own resurrection and then fulfill it. The fact of the empty tomb was not the result of some scheme to make His resurrection plausible. Any attempt to refute it is confronted with mounds of evidence, beginning with Christ's documented appearances.

After His resurrection, Jesus appeared many times to different people. Taking all four gospels and the other New Testament writings into account, here is a chronological ordering of the Lord's recorded post-resurrection appearances:

- Resurrection Sunday (Easter): to Mary Magdalene (John 20:14–18); to the women coming back from the tomb with the angels' message (Matthew 28:8–10); in the afternoon to Peter (Luke 24:34; 1 Corinthians 15:5); toward evening to the disciples on the road to Emmaus (Luke 24:13–31); to all the apostles except Thomas (Luke 24:36–43; John 20:19–24).

- Eight days later: to the apostles, including Thomas (John 20:24–29).

- In Galilee: at the Lake of Tiberias to the seven (John 21:1–23); to the apostles and five hundred others on a mountain (1 Corinthians 15:6).

- At Jerusalem and Bethany (a second time): to James (1 Corinthians 15:7); to the eleven (Matthew 28:16–20; Mark 16:14–20; Luke 24:33–53; Acts 1:3–12).

- To Paul: near Damascus (Acts 9:3–6; 1 Corinthians 15:8); in the temple (Acts 22:17–21; 23:11).

- To Stephen outside Jerusalem (Acts 7:55).

- To John on the island of Patmos (Revelation 1:10–19).

Stop for just a moment. Let the evidence you have just read sink in. Jesus only appeared to His followers. For the most part His appearances were infrequent, with only four after Easter and before His ascension (return to heaven). There was nothing fantastic or farfetched in His appearances, and they were all different in nature—in the places they occurred, the length of time involved, the words spoken, and even the mood of the apostles. All Christ's appearances were bodily in nature because Jesus wanted the disciples to be sure of this fact (Luke 24:39–40; John 20:27).

It's absolutely amazing to think that so many people, on different days and in distinct situations, all had encounters with the risen Christ. The resurrection of Christ means that God gave His approval to the claims and works of Jesus. These claims would have been sacrilegious if Jesus were not truly the Son of God. However, the Resurrection validates Jesus and His teaching. The empty tomb should assure us forever that all the things He taught were true. If Christ had not risen from the dead, then He wouldn't be alive to do all His post-resurrection work. We would not have an Advocate, Head of the church, or Intercessor. Ultimately, there'd be no living Person to live inside us and give us power (Romans 6:1–10; Galatians 2:20).

In the resurrected Christ we've got strength for today and hope for tomorrow.

Bear in mind, the religion of Christianity is not unique; it's Jesus Christ that sets it apart from all other religions. It's what you say and do with Jesus that ultimately is the key to your life's history and your eternal destiny.

WHAT ABOUT YOU?

Have you decided to become a follower of Jesus yet? To trust His word—the Bible—over everything you are reading and hearing about spirituality? What do you think about God now?

You may not completely understand how God places the penalty for your sin on Jesus. Few of us really understand just how much we have been forgiven. But you don't need to understand everything all at once. God only asks you to believe and take the first step.

No one totally understands electricity. Scientists talk about it as a fundamental entity of all matter. They can create electrical charges and harness electricity to use. But as a scientist once said, "Electricity in its essence is quite unexplainable." Even though we can't completely understand electricity, that doesn't stop us from using it.

When you decide to become a Christian, you may not totally understand everything to start with. But as you read the Bible and allow God to teach you, your comprehension will grow. Keep in mind, this decision will be costly. It will cost you your favorite sins and your self-centered attitude to try to live your life without God. It may cost you some friends who don't understand why your life is so different. The decision to follow Jesus may even cost you your current dreams about the future, because God may have something planned for you that is totally different than you ever expected. The cost is high to accept Christ, but not anywhere near what it will cost you to reject Him.

If you're ready to start a relationship with Jesus Christ, take a few minutes right now and follow the steps listed below. It's a simple way to establish an intimate relationship with the living God. Becoming a follower of Jesus Christ is the most important decision you will ever make in life. There's nothing greater than experiencing God's love, forgiveness, and acceptance. Once you've made the decision to follow Jesus, life takes on a whole new meaning.

HOW YOU CAN EXPERIENCE A RELATIONSHIP WITH GOD[16]

1. God's Purpose: Peace and Life

God loves you and wants you to experience peace and life—satisfying and eternal.

"Therefore, since we have been made right in God's sight by faith, we have peace with God because of what Jesus Christ our Lord has done for us" (Romans 5:1).

"For God so loved the world that he gave his only Son, so that everyone who believes in him will not perish but have eternal life" (John 3:16).

So why don't most people have this peace and abundant life that God planned for us to possess?

2. The Problem: Our Separation

God created us in His own image to experience a meaningful and satisfying life. He did not make us like robots to automatically love and obey Him.

---

[16]Adapted from "Steps to Peace with God," (World Wide Publications). Used with permission from the Billy Graham Evangelistic Association.

God gave us a will and the freedom of choice. We chose to disobey God and go our own willful way. We still make this choice today. This results in separation from God.

"For all have sinned; all fall short of God's glorious standard" (Romans 3:23).

"For the wages of sin is death, but the free gift of God is eternal life through Christ Jesus our Lord" (Romans 6:23).

Our choice results in separation from God. People have tried in many ways to bridge this gap between themselves and God. Our attempts to reach God include doing good things, religion, philosophy, and morality.

"There is a path before each person that seems right, but it ends in death" (Proverbs 14:12).

"Your sins have cut you off from God. Because of your sin, he has turned away and will not listen anymore" (Isaiah 59:2).

No bridge reaches God . . . except one.

3. God's Bridge: The Cross

Jesus Christ died on the cross and rose from the grave. He paid the penalty for our sin and bridged the gap between God and people.

"For there is only one God and one Mediator who can reconcile God and people. He is the man Christ Jesus" (1 Timothy 2:5).

"Christ also suffered when he died for our sins once for all time. He never sinned, but he died for sinners that he might bring us safely home to God. He suffered physical death, but he was raised to life in the Spirit" (1 Peter 3:18).

"But God showed his great love for us by sending Christ to die for us while we were still sinners" (Romans 5:8).

God has provided the only way, and every person must make a choice.

4. Our Response: Receive Christ

We have to trust Jesus Christ as Lord and Savior and receive Him by personal invitation.

"If you confess with your mouth that Jesus is Lord and believe in your heart that God raised him from the dead, you will be saved" (Romans 10:9).

"Look! Here I stand at the door and knock. If you hear me calling and open the door, I will come in, and we will share a meal as friends" (Revelation 3:20).

"But to all who believed him and accepted him, he gave the right to become children of God" (John 1:12).

Here's how you can start a relationship with Jesus (become a Christian):

1. Admit that you are a sinner.
2. Be willing to turn away from your sins (repent).
3. Believe that Jesus Christ died for you on the cross and rose from the grave.
4. Through prayer, invite Jesus Christ to come in and be in charge of your life through the Holy Spirit (receive Him as Lord and Savior).

Pray something like this:

Dear Jesus,

I know that I have sinned and need your forgiveness. I now turn from my sins to follow you. I believe that you died on the cross to take the punishment for my sins and that you came back to life after three days. I surrender my heart and life to you. I want you to be my Savior and follow you as Lord. Thank you for your love and for the gift of eternal life.

In Jesus' name. Amen.

Have you decided to establish a relationship with Jesus? If so, you've made the most important decision of your life! If you have sincerely accepted Jesus, then you can trust Him. Check out what the Bible says in Romans 10:13 (NIV): "Everyone who calls on the name of the Lord will be saved."

When we surrender our lives to Jesus, we become brand-new people. Check out the promise in 2 Corinthians 5:17: "What this means is that those who become Christians become new persons. They are not the same anymore, for the old life is gone. A new life has begun!" The

Holy Spirit gives us new life and we're not the same anymore. We are not rehabilitated or reeducated. Instead, we are new creations living in vital union with Jesus (see Colossians 2:6–7). A supernatural conversion takes place the moment we accept Christ. We don't just change some stuff in our life, we start a new life under a new Master.

This is something that Wicca does not offer. But there's a catch: In order to get this new life, you have to surrender the old one. You must give up control, which is opposite to the teachings of Wicca. And this is opposite of what our culture says. *Surrender* is a negative word because we are told the way to freedom and becoming an individual is staying in charge. That's why Wicca is so popular today—because people not only make their own deities, they are the god of their own life.

When it comes to Jesus and the kingdom of God, things are just the opposite. Jesus told His followers in Matthew 16:25, "If you try to keep your life for yourself, you will lose it. But if you give up your life for me, you will find true life." Surrendering to someone else is always hard because you no longer maintain control. But God is not just anyone—He is the One who made you and knows what is best for you. The only way we can experience real purpose in our life, as well as wisdom for the tough stuff we face, is by surrendering our lives to Jesus.

This relationship that you have established is one that cannot be broken or terminated. Jesus promises to never let you down and never give you up (Hebrews 13:5). This is the core of Christianity. It's not a religion; it's God revealing himself to us, rescuing us from our sin, and making it possible for us to experience a relationship with Him.

And just like you would do in any other relationship, remember to stay in touch with your new best friend. You can do this in a couple of ways. Start by reading the letters Jesus has already given you telling about who He is, how He can help you, how to live your life, and most of all how much He loves you. All this and much more is found in the Bible. Take time each day to read and study a portion of it. And just like you might instant-message a friend on the Internet, you can send an instant message to God through prayer. You can pray anytime, anyplace, and you don't even have to be online!

Make sure you get plugged in to a church where they teach about

Jesus, from the Bible, and where you can worship and develop friendships with other Christians. Remember to tell others what Jesus has done for you, because they can experience the same thing. And look for ways to serve God by helping others in need in the world.

You may feel totally different now or you may not. The most important thing is that you now know how you can start a relationship with the living God, and you will have the rest of eternity to develop and experience it!

And by the way, if you did say a prayer to place your faith and trust in Jesus Christ, please let me know by using the contact information in the back of this book. This is just the beginning of a great new life with Jesus. I want to pray for you and send you some things to help you get started growing in this new relationship with God.

ONE FINAL THOUGHT

The most important question you will ever answer is, "Who is Jesus?" I've tried to give as much information as possible for you to be able to answer this question. Take your time. Give very careful and thoughtful attention to what we've discussed in this book. Don't take my word for it—examine the facts. Check out the evidence for yourself.

Scott Cunningham passed from this life after a long illness. If it were possible to speak with him today, I wonder what he would say to us about spirituality. I question whether or not he would change the dedication in one of his books that reads: "This book is dedicated to the forces that watch over and guide us—however we may envision or name them." What would Scott say about God now?

Jesus made the first choice—to love and to die for us, to invite us to live with Him forever. We make the next choice—to accept or reject His offer. Without His choice, we would have no choice to make. Now it's up to you: Whose word you gonna trust?

CHAPTER ELEVEN

WHEN A FRIEND IS IN WICCA

AMANDA DIDN'T REALIZE HOW ENTICING witchcraft could be. "I saw the movie *The Craft* and was instantly hooked." She grew up in a Christian home and knew it was wrong, but she wanted to know more about it. Amanda started studying Wicca and became involved for several months. She began doubting God and questioned her relationship with Him. Amanda still went to church every Sunday but basically zoned out and wasn't paying attention. "My life basically just went down the drain." At a weekend retreat with her church youth group, she realized what was happening to her and came back to God. When Amanda got home she threw away everything she owned that had to do with Wicca. "When I think how far I separated myself from God, I get goose bumps. It's scary to be away from His love."

Jake was a Wiccan for two years, but with the help of a friend and a Bible study he attended, he found Christ. "I realized that Wicca was not fulfilling my spiritual needs. I was not sure how to break away and go to the God who loves me." But a friend helped him see the love and benefits that living with Jesus could give.

Do you know someone like Jake or Amanda? What can we do to

help those we care about who are involved in Wicca and witchcraft—a religion that denies that Jesus is God? All around us are friends, family members, neighbors, and people at school who are living in spiritual darkness. The devil has done a masterful job at getting them to believe his lies. "Satan, the god of this evil world, has blinded the minds of those who don't believe, so they are unable to see the glorious light of the Good News that is shining upon them. They don't understand the message we preach about the glory of Christ, who is the exact likeness of God" (2 Corinthians 4:4).

Be careful that you don't underestimate the deceptive power of Wicca—even if you claim to be a follower of Jesus. Seventeen-year-old Sara calls herself a hardcore Christian and says she's extremely active in her church and youth group. But when it comes to Wicca, she's bought the lie. "My attitude toward Wicca is that it really doesn't mean anything. It is totally fake. I don't think it is good, but it is not bad either. It really doesn't do anything."

Those involved in Wicca have bought the lie of religion that says you can get to heaven—or however you describe life after death—through your own efforts and in your own way. Let's face it, that's an easy trap to fall into. We are so used to earning things, working for things. Even as little children we are taught that if we do a certain thing we will be rewarded. We then want to carry this over to religion. It's hard to imagine that something as significant as eternal life is a free gift from God. Of course, Satan complicates matters with his lies, and unfortunately many people believe him. You and I have the privilege of rescuing these spiritual hostages of the enemy (2 Timothy 2:26).

WARNING SIGNS

How can we recognize if a friend is involved in Wicca and practicing witchcraft? Here are some potential warning signs to look for:

1. *Withdrawal from routine activities*—the normal everyday stuff. Beware of unusual seclusion or secrecy by your friend.
2. *Obsession with death and suicide.* Many who practice Wicca believe in reincarnation. Pay attention to the music your friend is listening to and the DVDs they are watching—and anything

else they're feeding their mind. Also look for any doodles or scribbles on a notebook or book cover with these themes.

3. *Fixation with Wiccan symbols and runes.* These symbols can be found in and on a variety of items, including a Book of Shadows and correspondence. Runes are symbols that when drawn, painted, traced, carved, or visualized are believed to release specific energies.[1] Many of these symbols are explained in Appendix D.

4. *Possession of Wiccan, Pagan, and Shamanistic publications.* These could be in the form of books, newsletters, magazines, and tabloids. Topics and content could include poetry, spells, songs, rituals, herb craft, artwork, etc.

5. *Excessive fears or anxiety.* If your friend exhibits unusual preoccupation and paranoia about current events in the world situation, at school, or at home, then you have a reason to be concerned.

6. *Fascination with or possession of unique knives.* The magick knife (or athame) is often dull, usually double-edged, with a dark or black handle. It isn't used for cutting purposes in Wicca, but to direct energy during rites and spells. The white-handled knife (sometimes called a bolline) is simply a practical working knife. It is used to cut wands or sacred herbs, inscribe symbols onto candles or wood, clay or wax, and in cutting cords for use in magick. It is usually white-handled to distinguish it from the magick knife.[2]

7. *Book of Shadows.* This is a Wiccan workbook containing invocations, ritual patterns, rules governing magick, etc. It's much like a diary.

8. *Altars.* They can be simple or extremely elaborate, and located in a bedroom closet, basement, garage, or attic. Usually they are placed with a witch's circle, which is considered sacred space. They can have candles, incense, photographs, or even personal effects on them. It all depends on the function of the magick to be performed.

Keep in mind that just because you observe one or more of these

[1]Scott Cunningham, *Wicca: A Guide for the Solitary Practitioner* (St. Paul: Llewellyn Publications, 2003), 177.
[2]Ibid., 30–31.

signs in a friend's life, it does not mean that they are involved in Wicca. But it could mean that they are facing some tough issues and need some help.

PRACTICAL TIPS

To rescue someone from Wicca or another form of spiritual darkness, we must first fully understand the level of commitment and preparation that must be in place in our own lives. Like all good soldiers, we must be prepared for battle. Let's look at some practical things we need to remember as we tell our friends who are involved in Wicca and witchcraft about Jesus.

1. Approach your friend gradually. You need to be aware of what your friend believes and try to understand where they are coming from. Be patient and take them one step at a time closer to an understanding of what it really means to have a relationship with Jesus.

2. Try to find out what unmet need in your friend's life seems to be met in Wicca. That can be a starting point for telling them how Jesus has met this need in your own life—or someone else you know—and how He can do the same for them.

3. Be sensitive to your friend's perspective. Don't make fun of their involvement in Wicca, as illogical as it may seem. This will only cause them to avoid discussing their "religion" with you.

4. Try to find common ground with them. Ask questions about the way they personally practice Wicca to see what might be similar to Christianity. Remember, most Wiccans are solitary practitioners. Establishing common ground can be a great starting point for discussion. It could be things like
   - living a moral life
   - environmental issues
   - finding personal peace
   - the importance of self-discipline
   - concern for gender equality
   - prayer and meditation
   - what God is like
   - the source of power

5. Highlight the differences between Wicca and Christianity. (See the comparison guide in the last chapter—"Conclusion: Which Spiritual Path?") Most people involved in Wicca have never really heard the truth about what Christians believe. Check out the comparisons between Wicca and Christianity in the next chapter for some help.

6. Clarify terms and definitions. Familiarize yourself with Wiccan terms. Check out the glossary in Appendix B. But remember, you don't need to expose yourself to witchcraft to effectively help lead someone out of it.

7. Show by example your trust in God alone. Help your friend see that the only source of security, acceptance, and significance in this world is found in a relationship with Jesus Christ.

8. Be open about your faith in a personal God, not some "force," god and goddess, or a self-made deity. Emphasize the benefits of a relationship with a personal God. Things like

   - He is able to love us,
   - He can hear and answer our prayers,
   - He comforts and helps us in powerful ways when we're hurting.

   And remember that it's also important for you to share with your friend how you define God.

9. Clearly explain the reality of sin and how God has provided the way of forgiveness—complete and total forgiveness—found absolutely nowhere else. Only Jesus paid for our sin and then defeated death by resurrection.

10. Use the Bible strategically to explain and support what you believe. Make sure that personal study of the Bible is a priority in your life. Unfortunately, most Christians are not equipped to respond biblically when talking with those involved in Wicca and witchcraft. Make sure you can share with your friend why you believe the Bible is God's word and what evidence you have to support that it's true.

We're involved in a battle for truth, not power. We must help our friends and family to accept God's truth in their lives and stop believing the lies that Satan has fed their minds. Satan's only power is in his deceptive lies. The light of God's truth shatters the lies of the devil and sets us free to be the people God designed us to be.

11. Pray for and with your friend—with their permission.
12. Focus on Jesus. It all comes down to who you believe Jesus is; that's why it's important to point to Him as much as possible. Help your friend see that He is more than a prophet, a good teacher, or just a man. He is God. And remember to help your friend understand that
    - the All and Jesus both can't be right;
    - the god/goddess and Jesus both can't be right;
    - self-made deities and Jesus all can't be right.

    Encourage your friend to read the New Testament books of Mark and John, so they learn more about the life and work of Jesus. Jesus is unique. There is no other religious leader like Him—never has been and never will be. If we have a relationship with Jesus, we have been given the awesome responsibility to tell others the good news of salvation through Him. It is singularly the most important information in history because it offers the truth of the only door to heaven and fulfillment here on earth. Jesus said, "I am the way, the truth, and the life. No one can come to the Father except through me" (John 14:6).

Remember that your ultimate goal is for your friend to be freed from the spiritual darkness of Wicca and place their faith and trust in Jesus. But this may take some time. Be patient and never lose sight of your goal. Ask questions about their beliefs and respond in a caring way. Don't forget the unseen spiritual battle mentioned in Ephesians 6 that we are all involved in. We battle a fierce enemy, but one who was critically wounded when Jesus died on the cross. Don't forget, God cares about your friend even more than you do. So don't give up hope!

GOD USES PEOPLE LIKE YOU

Throughout history God has used people just like you to change the course of history. Have you ever asked God to use you as a light in the darkness of your home, neighborhood, campus, and in your world? No matter how old you are or what weaknesses you may have, don't let anyone put you down or make you feel like God can't use you.

Instead, remember what the Bible says in 1 Timothy 4:12: "Don't let anyone think less of you because you are young. Be an example to all believers in what you teach, in the way you live, in your love, your faith, and your purity."

I owe my life to someone just like you. And that's why I'm so committed to helping teenagers be all that God designed them to be. Robbie was taking drum lessons from me while I was still in the music industry. Each week during his lesson he would tell me about his best friend. He told me how he shared everything with this friend, but he never told me his best friend's name. I actually started to become jealous of Robbie and this relationship he had with his best friend, because I didn't have a friend like he did. One day before the lesson started, I finally asked Robbie what his best friend's name was. His response just about knocked me over. "Jesus!" Rob said. "And He can be your best friend, too." It wasn't long afterward that I met Robbie's aunt and uncle, Billy and Danielle, who were Christians and entertainers in Hollywood, and they helped me put my faith and trust in Jesus.

As a result of one teenager's courage to tell me about his "best friend," people across the United States and in twenty-three foreign countries have heard the message of God's love through our ministry.

God used a teenager in my life and He wants to work through you, too. As you become aware of the spiritual condition of those around you, ask God how He wants to use you to help that person find answers in a relationship with Jesus. He said, "You are the light of the world—like a city on a mountain, glowing in the night for all to see. Don't hide your light under a basket! Instead, put it on a stand and let it shine for all" (Matthew 5:14–15). One person really can make a difference in the world!

CONCLUSION:
WHICH SPIRITUAL PATH?

JESSICA AND HER FAMILY MOVED to Colorado when she was thirteen. They got really involved in an evangelical Christian church, and her parents signed her up for a Bible study so she could understand her faith better. Instead, she felt like all she learned about was how intolerant her church was. Jessica had a hard time when she felt like they railed against homosexuals and taught that people of different religions were damned. "This wasn't the Christianity I'd practiced before—how could my parents want me to be part of this?"[1]

She continued to go to church with her parents because she felt like she had no choice. Jessica felt empty inside sitting in the pew each week listening to the pastor talk about who's going to hell. One day when she was fifteen, she found a book called *Exploring Wicca* at a local bookstore. Since she was doubting her own religion, Jessica was curious to read it. By the time she finished the book that afternoon, she wanted to start practic-

---

[1] As told to Zoe C. Courtman, "My Religion Isn't Evil," *Seventeen* magazine, February 2005, 71.

ing Wicca, but Jessica knew her parents would disapprove.

So she hid her interest in Wicca from them because she didn't know how to tell them. After she came home from church, she would go to her room and secretly practice spells and rituals. "And as I did that, this calming energy would flow through me. It was the feeling I'd always imagined I should be feeling when I was in church—but never did."[2]

After about three months, Jessica finally decided to be open about her involvement in Wicca. But she was still scared to tell her parents. One day she came home wearing a pentacle—a ritual object containing the witch's symbol (pentagram) with a circle around it. Jessica's mom got angry and demanded she take off the "evil" necklace immediately. Jessica screamed, "Why are you trying to push your religion on me? I don't want to go to your church anymore."[3] Her mother told her that she'd lose her car, her family, and everything that goes with it if she left their church.

"It was hard, but I found such solace in Wicca that I couldn't give it up for my parents. And I hoped they'd eventually accept it—I mean, it was a part of me. But I was wrong. I only escaped the tension this year, when I left home for college."[4]

Unfortunately, Jessica's not alone in her struggles to make sense out of spirituality and live at peace with her parents. She's also not the only teen who wrestles with doubts about her faith and has gotten caught up in the lie of "relative truth" in our culture. And let's face it, Jessica's not the only teen who's had a bad experience at church. Even superstars go through tough times as teenagers. Punk princess Avril Lavigne, for example, strayed from her parents' strict Christian standards and now writes music that reflects the ups and downs she experienced as a teen.

But as sincere and nice as Jessica sounds, she's definitely confused because she's bought some deceptive spiritual lies. I've lost count how many times I've heard someone say how intolerant Christianity is, how we need to be more accepting of people, and how we Christians should practice "loving our neighbor" more, like the Bible says.

A lot of people today think this way. Society says we have to be

_____
[2]Ibid.
[3]Ibid.
[4]Ibid.

politically correct and tolerant. People feel the need to affirm all belief systems and avoid giving claim to any single religion as the true one. The thinking process goes something like this: All religions are equally true and all deserve the same validation. Plus, it's not good to close your mind to vast areas of human experience and knowledge. Based on this kind of thinking, you don't have to make any hard decisions that involve a change of lifestyle. You can believe in everything and nothing—all at the same time—without any responsibility.

In a magazine article I wrote, I said that Wicca and Christianity both couldn't be right. Just that comment alone resulted in a bunch of letters from teens and adults telling me how wrong I was and how I shouldn't judge other religions. A seventeen-year-old girl who called herself "Ms. Farrell" was one of the people who sent an e-mail. Here's part of her comments:

"You state that both religions (Wicca and Christianity) can't be true. Is it not possible that one God, who created everything, created multiple religions because He or She knew that not everyone would agree on one set framework, because they gave us choice? Thank you for your time. I did not mean this as an insult to your religion. I respect you and I am very glad that you, unlike many others, have found something to believe in as I have."

DOESN'T BEING SINCERE COUNT?

Some people think it doesn't matter what you believe, as long as you're sincere. Ms. Farrell certainly sounds sincere in her beliefs, but being sincere isn't enough. A lot of people are sincere in what they believe. Centuries ago people sincerely believed that the gods at war caused thunder. We now know that their sincere belief was superstition. At one time people also believed that the sun went around the earth until Galileo demonstrated that this was not true. Once again a sincere belief was not enough. People can be very sincere in what they believe, but they can be sincerely wrong. Just look at the terrorists who carry out their missions in the Middle East. There's no question that they are sincere in what they believe, but they are dreadfully wrong.

Don't forget that sincerity is important in our relationships with others. No one likes a hypocrite. But just being sincere isn't enough. I'm always amazed at how people so often say that sincerity is all you need when it comes to religion, but not to other dimensions of life. Stop and think for a minute. You would never say this about a historical event like World War II. You may sincerely believe that Hitler actually won, but you'd be wrong. You'd never apply this kind of thinking to mathematics. No one in their right mind would say that if they sincerely believed hard enough, one plus one equals three. Why do we do this when it comes to religion and not with other things?

Maybe because it can be hard to be absolutely sure when it comes to religion. Or maybe we're more concerned with actions rather than philosophy. On the other hand, it could be because religion is about ultimate issues like life and death. And when you get right down to it, no one really wants to look at them very closely. We'd rather live for today and not be too worried about tomorrow. It's a lot easier to be sincere, do the best you can to live a good life, and hope it will all count for something in the end.

Let's look at the issue of sincerity in another way. The things Jesus taught and those taught by Wiccans point in very different directions. You might sincerely think that Jesus was just a good man, and you might sincerely be practicing the craft. But what happens if you are sincerely wrong in the end?

AREN'T ALL RELIGIONS BASICALLY THE SAME?

Cherie says she was raised as a Christian, but as she got older she felt like she'd been brainwashed as a child with something other than the truth. She's convinced that once you truly understand witchcraft, Wiccans, and pagans, you'll know that their beliefs in general are not much different than Christians'. Cherie says since most religions carry the same stories like "the great flood," they're all basically the same. But she still thinks that most Christians are very closed-minded, brainwashed individuals who basically believe that "if you don't believe the way I believe, you are wrong and will go to hell." That's why when she has children of her own, they will be allowed to decide for themselves what they choose to believe—a choice she claims she was not given by the Christians in her life.

Jarred is a Wiccan and gets offended when anyone puts down his religion. It's one he claims few people truly understand—especially Christians, who he thinks are extremely narrow-minded. He says most Christians also go against the teachings of their God, who tells people to "love thy neighbor," because the only religion he ever hears about that is persecuting others is Christians. Jarred says, "Wiccans are not self-centered, we strive to help others more than we do ourselves, and we follow a path of belief that is far more conceivable than those of other religions."

Kerrie was raised Lutheran when she was young, but at fifteen converted to paganism. "Steve, do you really think that there is one way of thinking for everyone? Wicca does not preach that everyone who is not Wiccan is wrong. We accept all religions. I am grateful for my Christian upbringing, as it gave me a cornerstone on which to build my beliefs." Kerrie thinks it's important to teach that we should accept and love everyone else. She goes on to ask, "Why teach that all who are not like you are wrong?" She says she's not a typical Wiccan because she does not believe in more than one deity. "I prefer to think of the deity as a goddess because I love the nurturing, tender qualities associated with females and mothers," Kerrie tells me.

Cherie's, Jarred's, and Kerrie's views are definitely politically correct in our "relative truth culture." Plus, if you compare different religions, on the surface, many seem to have similar moral and ethical principles. So doesn't that basically mean you can take any spiritual path you choose? Even significant thinkers throughout history have held to this common-sense view. Mahatma Gandhi said, "The soul of religion is one, but it is encased in a multitude of forms." As appealing as this way of thinking might be, it won't work.

But just ask those who are actually involved in witchcraft and Christianity if the two are basically the same. They'll all give you a definite NO. Christians are definitely different from Wiccans.

Notice how they have absolutely opposing views of what God is really like. For example, the idea of Wiccan deities has been compared to a family tree, with the All, or universal energy, at the top. The god and goddess (lord and lady) are the next in line, symbolizing the perfectly balanced male and female aspects of divinity. Finally, closest to humans on earth are the myriad of deities custom-designed to fit your personal taste. And just like you might choose a friend based on things that you were drawn to instinctively or emotionally, so you can also choose your favorite traits for your special god or goddess.

Then look at the concept of belief in a personal God—there's agreement on if and how He shows himself to us. Followers of Jesus believe that God not only reveals himself to us, but He also reveals His will. He did it in the only language that we could fully understand—in a human life—through Jesus. That's what Christmas is all about.

God wanted to communicate with us more effectively. Imagine you're watching a farmer plow a field. You notice that the farmer on his tractor will plow under an anthill next time around. Because you love ants, you run to the anthill to warn its tiny inhabitants. First you shout to them the impending danger, but they continue their work. You then try many other forms of communication, but nothing seems to get through to the imperiled ants. You soon realize that the only way you can really reach them is by becoming one of them. Christians believe that throughout human history, God has used numerous means of communication to reach humanity with His message. He finally sent His Son into the world.

The most significant difference is how we make ourselves acceptable to God. Wicca stresses that by following their teachings, you can be fulfilled in life and eventually reach perfection after you die. This involves a form of karma (cause and effect, paying off your guilt) and reincarnation. But this is miles apart from God's total and complete forgiveness that makes everlasting life possible without having to work for it. The Bible teaches that no one is capable of making himself or herself acceptable to God. But the God of Christianity is personal, and because of His awesome love for humanity, He wants to have a relationship with us and makes this possible through Jesus' death on the cross.

DON'T WICCA AND CHRISTIANITY BOTH LEAD TO GOD?

While it may be politically correct to say that Wicca and Christianity both lead to God, it's just not possible. If you start closely examining the beliefs, you will see that their essential concepts—God, truth, reality, the basic problem of humanity and its solution—are very different.

Sometimes they actually contradict each other.

How can Wicca and Christianity both lead to God when they have such different beliefs about God and life after death? We don't need a religion; we need a relationship with the living God. Christianity isn't about people in search of God, but rather God in search of people.

Check out the comparison guide of Wicca/witchcraft and Christianity below and see for yourself.

- Most Wiccans believe in some form of reincarnation.[5] For witches, reincarnation is different from what a Buddhist or Hindu believes. Instead of an endless karma, witches view reincarnation as something positive that takes the soul upward in its advancement toward godhood.[6] Christians do not believe there are additional chances to come back and keep advancing your soul to new levels. The Bible is very clear when it says we die only once and then we are judged (Hebrews 9:26–28; 2 Peter 2:9).

- Wiccans believe they can influence reality through invoking invisible spirits and powers. They believe that magick is the craft of witchcraft.[7] Using magick, witchcraft, or invisible spirits is detestable to God and something He will not tolerate (Deuteronomy 18:9–13; Isaiah 8:19).

- The Wiccan view of salvation can be summed up with this statement: "We can open new eyes and see that there is nothing to be saved from; no struggle of life against the universe, no God outside the world to be feared and obeyed."[8] Christians believe that we are all born with a spiritual terminal disease called sin that causes us to disobey God and go our own willful way. This causes us to be separated from God. The remedy was Christ's death on the cross (Romans 3:23, 6:23; Isaiah 59:2; 1 Timothy 2:5; 1 Peter 3:18).

- Wiccans believe that experience is a more important revelation than any code of belief, and that it's more important to reveal your own truth than to rely on doctrine. Christians believe that the most

---

[5]Starhawk, *The Spiral Dance: A Rebirth of the Ancient Religions of the Great Goddess* (San Francisco: Harper & Row, 1979), 84.

[6]Ceisiwr Serith, *The Pagan Family: Handing the Old Ways Down* (St. Paul: Llewellyn Publications, 1994), 198.

[7]Starhawk, 13, 109.

[8]Ibid., 14.

important revelation of truth is the Bible (Psalm 119:47, 72, 97; 2 Timothy 3:16; Hebrews 4:12).

- Wiccans worship the earth and creation. They recognize the divinity of nature and all living things.[9] Christians believe in worshiping the Creator, not the creation (Deuteronomy 4:39; Romans 1:25; Jude 25).

- Wiccans believe that people have their own divine nature: "Thou art Goddess, thou art God."[10] Christians believe that even though we are created in God's image, humanity is still sinful and fallen (Genesis 1:26–27; Romans 5:12). The Bible clearly teaches that all kinds of wickedness come from within a person, not some type of divinity (Jeremiah 17:9; Mark 7:14–23).

- Wiccans do not believe that Jesus was God in the flesh or Creator of the universe. They view Jesus as "a great white witch who knew the Coven of Thirteen."[11] The key principle that sets Christianity apart from any other religion is the belief that Jesus is God. One of the names for Jesus in the Bible is Immanuel, which means "God with us" (Matthew 1:21–23; John 1:1, 14, 18, 8:24; Philippians 2:5–6).

BEYOND TOLERANCE TO TRUTH

I've had many teens contact me at *Life on the Edge—Live!* to tell me how intolerant I am to think that my religion is the only one that's got it all right. Unfortunately, they don't really understand what it means to "tolerate" something. To tolerate a belief, viewpoint, lifestyle, etc., means that you allow it to exist, even though you don't agree with it or like it. If I were truly intolerant, I would try to silence other points of view and eliminate them. But just because I disagree with someone doesn't mean I'm intolerant.

Speaking of being intolerant, I've noticed something as I travel across North America speaking on public junior high and senior high

---

[9]Prudence Jones and Caitlin Matthews, eds., *Voices From the Circle: The Heritage of Western Paganism* (Wellingborough, Northamptonshire, England: The Aquarian Press, 1990), 40.

[10]Margot Adler, *Drawing Down the Moon: Witches, Druids, Goddess-Worshippers, and Other Pagans in America Today* (Boston: Beacon Press, 1986), 9.

[11]Doreen Valienete, *An ABC of Witchcraft: Past and Present* (New York: St. Martin's Press, 1973), 14.

school campuses. Before most assemblies, school administrators remind me that I cannot talk to the student body about God, Jesus, or the Bible. Yet if my assembly contained references to Islam, Hinduism, Buddhism, any other religion, or even alternative lifestyles, I can openly talk about them. Isn't it interesting that in the midst of an era of "tolerance," there's such great intolerance toward Christianity and Jesus?

It's really not about tolerance; it's about truth—absolute truth. People want to find and experience truth today but don't know where to find it. That's one of the reasons that reality TV shows have become so popular—the search for something genuine in the confusing world in which we live. But this isn't a new question; people have been asking the same thing for centuries. Even those who were close to Jesus were dealing with similar questions because they were confused about life. Jesus gave His followers an answer that is just as relevant today as it was back then. "I am the way, the truth, and the life. No one can come to the Father except through me" (John 14:6). Talk about a bold statement—it's one that no other religious leader has had the courage to make. Jesus is saying that He is the ultimate foundation for experiencing satisfaction in life. He is also stating that He answers the greatest needs in our lives. The answer to the confusion and pain in life is not a formula but a personal relationship with the living God.

Jesus is not a person who shows the way; He is the *only* way to God. He is the only one who can make sense out of day-to-day living and eternal meaning in life. Jesus is the way because He is both God and man. Wiccans consistently argue that this is narrow-minded thinking. But in reality it's wide enough for everyone in the world—if they will accept it and stop worrying about how narrow it is. We should be grateful that we can be confident we have a sure way to get to God.

Jesus is also saying that He not only tells the truth, He is truth. And because He is God in the flesh, He is the complete revelation of God. Teens involved in Wicca have exchanged the truth for a lie. Philosophers say that truth is an idea; the Bible says truth is a person: Jesus. Truth by its very definition is narrow. For example, two plus two always equals four, not five. Truth is absolute in mathematics, and we should recognize it also in spirituality. Because Jesus is truth, He is completely reliable in what He says and does. We can completely trust Him.

Finally, Jesus is not just saying He is alive; He is the source of all life—from the lowest plant to the highest spiritual level. He can make this claim because He conquered death. Who or what can make this claim in Wicca? Jesus died on the cross to demonstrate the power of His life.

Jesus is the only way we can get to God. It's not being impolite, politically incorrect, or intolerant; it's simply stating absolute truth. Stop being ripped off by spiritual lies; start experiencing the difference Jesus can make in your life.

Ultimately, the truth is that there are two enormous reasons why Wicca and Christianity don't both lead to God: the awesomeness of God and the sinfulness of people. Some people who believe that more than one religion can lead to God use the illustration of a mountain with many roads going up to the top. They say it doesn't matter which one you take; any of them will get you to the top. This view is invalid; it doesn't work. An illustration that better describes the real situation is that of people trying to find their way through a maze. There are a lot of paths that lead us to dead ends and fail to get us out of the maze, but there's only one way out.[12]

CHOOSE WISELY

Like it or not we have to admit that all religions—including Wicca and Christianity—are not the same. The bottom line is there's no religion that leads to God, but Christianity contains the clearest presentation of who Jesus is.

The only path to God is not through religion but through a personal relationship with Jesus Christ. Jesus was unique because He was the only one who could bridge the gap between a holy God and sinful people. Honestly compare Jesus to all the other religious leaders in the world. When you do, there will be no doubt in your mind why you should choose to trust Him.

Follow God, reject spiritual lies, and make sure to help others come to know the truth in Christ.

---

[12]Michael Green, *But Don't All Religions Lead to God?* (Grand Rapids, MI: Baker Books, 2002), 24–25.

DISCUSSION QUESTIONS

These are questions that you can study by yourself or discuss with a group:

1. What do people at your school think about Wicca? Do you think their opinion is based on accurate information?
2. What Wiccan beliefs have you noticed showing up in movies, TV shows, or music? How about in books you have read?
3. What one thing do you find most interesting about Wicca and witchcraft? What about the thing you find most confusing about this religion?
4. What's the attraction for teenagers with Wicca? Why?
5. How is Wicca similar to Christianity?
6. What is the goal of Wicca and witchcraft?
7. Why do you think it is so popular today for people to design their own custom belief system?
8. What is the biggest barrier to helping someone in Wicca understand the real truth about Christianity?
9. Read 1 Timothy 4:1–2. How do these verses relate to Wicca and witchcraft? Be specific.
10. Have you ever known anyone who was deeply involved in Wicca and

witchcraft? How could you help someone like that?

11. If you could only share one specific difference to compare Wicca and Christianity with someone, what would it be and why?

12. There are a lot of places in the Bible where God talks specifically about the subject of witchcraft. Check out what He says in the following parts of the Bible:

- Deuteronomy 18:9–13
- Nahum 3:4
- 2 Kings 9:22
- Revelation 21:8
- Micah 5:12

13. If someone visited your youth group or campus club, would they feel loved and accepted? What can you do to help change things to the way they should be?

14. Why is it wrong for a Christian to believe in reincarnation? Find at least one verse in the Bible to support your answer.

15. Wiccans like to think of themselves as being active in trying to address the problems in the world. As Christians, we should be even more active in making a difference. What one thing can you do this week to help deal with a problem in your sphere of influence?

16. What is the difference between knowing about Jesus and really knowing Him? Be specific.

17. Explain in your own words how Jesus is unique and different from the Wiccan All, the god and goddess, and deities. What makes Him so special?

18. Who first told you about Jesus? How was He described to you? What about Him did you find appealing at first? What about now?

19. What areas of your life are the most difficult to surrender to God? Why?

20. Think of at least one person you know who needs to be rescued from Wicca and spiritual darkness. Take a few minutes to pray for that person, asking God how He wants to use you. Then think about what might be the best strategy you can use to reach him or her. Besides praying for this person, how else does God want you to help him or her?

21. What are the three most meaningful things you learned in this book? How do they apply to your life?

THE REDE AND
THE THREEFOLD LAW

WICCAN REDE

Bide ye the Wiccan laws ye must,
in perfect love and perfect trust.
Ye must live and let live,
fairly take and fairly give.
Cast the Circle thrice about,
to keep unwelcome spirits out.
To bind the spell well every time,
let the spell be spoken in rhyme.
Soft of eye and light of touch,
speak ye little and listen much.
Deosil go by waxing moon,
chanting out the Wiccan runes.
Widdershins go by waning moon,
chanting out the baneful tune.
When the Lady's moon is new,
kiss the hand to Her times two.

When the moon rides at Her peak,
then the heart's desire seek.
Heed the North wind's mighty gale:
lock the door and trim the sail.
When the wind comes from the South,
love will kiss thee on the mouth.
When the Moor wind blows from the West,
departed spirits have no rest.
When the wind blows from the East,
expect the new and set the feast.
Nine woods in the cauldron go,
burn then quick and burn them slow.
Elder be the Lady's tree,
burn it not or cursed ye'll be.
When the wheel begins to turn,
let the Beltane fires burn.
When the wheel as turned to Yule,
light the log and the Horned One rules.
Heed ye flower, bush and tree,
by the Lady, Blessed Be.
Where the rippling waters go,
cast a stone, the truth to know.
When ye have and hold a need,
hearken not to others' greed.
With a fool no seasons spend,
or be counted as his friend.
Merry meet and merry part,
bright the cheeks and warm the heart.
Mind the Threefold Law ye should,
three times bad and three times good.
When misfortune is enow,
wear the blue star on thy brow.
True in love ye must be,
lest thy love be false to thee.
These words the Wiccan Rede fulfill:
An ye harm none, do what ye will.[1]

---

[1] *The Rede Of The Wiccae* (*The Rede*) is commonly attributed to Lady Gwen (Gwynne) Thompson, a Celtic Traditionalist who submitted the poem as it was given to her by her grandmother, Adriana Porter.

Translation: You can basically do anything in the world that you want, as long as you don't perceive it to cause harm to yourself or anyone else.

THE THREEFOLD LAW

"Ensure that your actions are honorable, for all that you do shall return to you, threefold, good or bane."

Translation: If you do something nasty, eventually something three times as nasty will happen to you. If you do something good, eventually something three times as good will happen to you.

These are two basic beliefs that most Wiccans practice.

GLOSSARY OF WICCAN/ WITCHCRAFT TERMS

Affirmation. A positive, repetitive declaration about something you want to manifest in your life. It always needs to be in the positive and present form.

Akasha. A Sanskrit word used to describe the concept of Spirit. It's the fifth element—the omnipresent spiritual power that permeates the universe and unifies the other four elements (fire, water, earth, and air).

Akashic Records. Edgar Cayce, a noted psychic, developed the concept of a place on the astral plane where there's a huge collection of information on everyone who has ever lived and ever will live. Facts about people like who they were, what they accomplished, when they were born, and when they will die are found here.

Altar. A working surface, like a tabletop, that's to be used only for magickal or religious purposes. It can be round, square, triangular, oblong, or oval.

Amulet. An object that has been magickally empowered to protect you from a specific type of negative energy.

Animism. The concept that the entire earth is a living organism is a widespread belief in neopagan religions. The word *animism* means "soul" or "breath." Some witches even view animism as "the heart and soul" of ancient witchcraft. Some Wiccans even believe that matter like rocks are alive and that all objects in the universe have some kind of inner consciousness.

Archetype. Represents a character or set of human characteristics to all people throughout all cultures. It can also mean "original model," like the characters of a myth.

Astral Travel. The ability for the spirit to leave the body and visit other places and times.

Athame. A Wiccan ritual knife. It usually has a double-edged blade with a black handle. Most of the time it is used to direct personal power during ritual workings.

Augury. The art, ability, or practice of divination by signs and omens.

Aura. "Invisible breath." Witches see aura as a kind of energy atmosphere that surrounds each living thing.

Balefire. A bonfire or a smaller fire that is lit for magickal purposes.

Banishing Magick. Using your will to make something go away.

Beltane. A Wiccan Sabbat celebrated on April 30 or May 1. Beltane is also known as May Eve, Roodmas, Walpurgis Night, or Cethsamhain. Beltane celebrates the symbolic union of the goddess and god.

Besom. Broom.

Bind. To bind a spell is to complete its casting, releasing it to do its work independently of the weaver of the spell.

Binding. A binding spell ties up or restrains a person's negative behavior but not the person.

Blessing Way. An alternative to the conventional baby shower. This ritual offers nurture and support for the mother-to-be, prayers for the ease and safety of the birth, and prayers for the baby's health and good life.

Book of Shadows. A collection of spiritual lessons, spells, magickal rules, and other information that is written down in a journal as a reference book. No one true Book of Shadows exists; they are all relevant to their respective users. Each one is a personal record of the individual's progress and work.

Book of the Dead. An Egyptian treatise on the afterlife that includes hundreds of magickal instructions for everything from invocations to charms.

Caduceus. A wand or staff with two snakes twined around it. At the top of the wand is a pair of wings.

Cakes and Ale. The Wiccan communion that consists of a natural beverage and cake offered to each participant in a ritual.

Cauldron. Any three-legged pot, which many witches and Wiccans use to represent the threefold goddess.

Censer. A heat-proof container in which incense is burned. It symbolizes the element of air.

Ceremony of Initiation. A ceremony of honor conducted by a group welcoming an initiate into the craft.

Chakra. Means "wheel" in Sanskrit. They are round, spinning discs of energy that lie along the spine from the tailbone to the top of the head. Taoists, Hindus, Hopis, and Tibetans all use chakra systems to explain different energies in the body.

Chalice. A drinking vessel, generally handle-less and comprising a bowl, stem, and base, used in Wicca to represent the element of water.

Chant. A series of meaningful words that the witch repeats to focus his or her will and raise energy toward a specific goal.

Charge. To infuse an object with personal power. An act of magick.

Charm. An object that a person associates with luck or another form of protection.

Cingulam. A knotted cord worn with ritual robes; it often denotes connection to a coven or degreed status.

Circle. A space marked out and consecrated by a witch or witches for the purposes of protection or a ritual.

Clairvoyance. Literally means "clear-seeing" and describes the ability of an individual to sense messages or visions using means other than the five human senses.

Cone of Power. A combination of love, creativity, and spirit that forms the basis of a witch's power. He or she then uses this energy to accomplish a desire.

Conscious Mind. That part of our minds at work while we perform acts related to the physical world.

Coven. A group of witches, usually centered on one or two leaders, who practice their religion together. The word most likely comes from the Middle English word *covent*, which means "a gathering."

Craft. Wicca, witchcraft, folk magick. Among other things, it is the art of using witchcraft power to influence future events. The word comes from "witch" (a wise one) and "craft" (strength and skill).

Crone. The third and eldest aspect of the goddess.

Crucible. A container made to heat metal at a high temperature. Also defined as a test or a trial.

Crystal. A stone with a particular, regular molecular structure. For magickal purposes it's not necessary to make a distinction between crystals and other minerals.

Curse. An appeal to supernatural powers for injury or harm to another.

Dark Ages. An era from about A.D. 476 to about the year 1000 characterized by repression and un-enlightenment.

Dedication. An individual's statement, through ceremony, that affirms his or her dedication to craft laws, structure, and to deity.

De-magicking. The process of returning magickal energies back to the earth.

Deosil. A clockwise motion, or the direction in which the shadow on a sundial moves as the sun "moves" across the sky. In the Wiccan dance, deosil is thought to generate energy with positive qualities.

Devas. A natural order of spirits (like fairies) with elemental essence.

Diabolism. The invocation of devils.

Divination. The magickal art of discovering the unknown by interpreting random patterns or symbols. Tools such as clouds, tarot cards, flames, or smoke are used. Divination contacts the psychic mind by tricking or drowsing the conscious mind through ritual and by observing or manipulating tools.

Druid. A priest or priestess of Celtic Europe who carried out social and religious functions.

Eclectic Witchcraft. An individual approach in which a witch picks and chooses from many different traditions and creates a personalized form of witchcraft that meets his or her needs and abilities.

Elements. Earth, air, fire, water. These four essences are the building blocks of the universe. Everything that exists or has the potential to exist contains one or more of these energies.

Elementals. The beings that live within the energy force of a specific element.

Elixir. A kind of potion used to energize, improve, and restore overall health to the person drinking it.

Ephemeris. A book that shows where the planets are every day of the year. Before computers, astrologers would use this and a lot of brain power to calculate charts.

Equinox. Means "equal night." Twice a year, the duration of daylight and night are equal. This is a traditional time for many Wiccan celebrations, marking two of the major points on the Wheel of the Year.

Esbat. A Wiccan ritual usually occurring on the full moon and dedicated to the goddess in her lunar aspect.

ESP. Extrasensory perception encompasses most paranormal abilities such as telepathy and clairvoyance.

Evocation. Calling up spirits or other non-physical entities to either visible appearance or invisible attendance. This is not necessarily a Wiccan practice. Compare with *invocation*.

Evoke. What witches do when they project energy from within themselves out into the universe.

Eye of Newt. The newt is related to the salamander. The incorporation of the eye refers to vision. The term means, "to receive supernatural foresight."

Fairy Dust. A super-fine glitter, similar to embossing powder. Some people buy it in vials, keep the vials closed, and wear them as magickal jewelry.

Familiar. An animal that acts in the capacity of a magickal partner, guide, and teacher to a witch.

Fetish. An object believed to have a specific magickal power for which that object is then carried, buried, burned, or otherwise utilized magickally.

Fire Festivals. First consisting of Beltane and Samhain, Imbolc and Lammas were added at a later date. These four festivals are associated with planting, harvesting, and hunting ceremonies.

Folk Magic. The magic of the people. The practice of projecting personal power, as well as the energies within natural objects such as herbs and crystals, to bring about needed change.

Goddess Mother. A Wiccan godmother.

Great Rite. A celebration of the god and goddess in literal or figurative terms so that the two can be united to create balance and increased power for magick.

Green Man. An image of the god aspect of divinity that is strongly connected with nature.

Group Mind. The establishing of perfect love and perfect trust among a group of individuals.

Handfasting. A Wiccan marriage ceremony. A couple (man and woman, two men, two women) is joined together for as long as their love shall last. If they decide they no longer love each other, they can split.

Hex/hexing. Derived from a German word for *witch*, describing the casting of a spell. Used synonymously with curse.

Higher Self. A spiritual part of humankind that has access to the universal mind and all the knowledge and wisdom of our past lives.

High Priest and Priestess. Individuals who have advanced knowledge of witchcraft and lead a coven.

Image Candle. A candle infused with a witch's unmatched energy, personality, and power.

Incantation. A chant with the intention of bringing magick into one's life.

Imbolc. A Wiccan Sabbat celebrated on February 2, also known as Candlemas, Lupercalia, Feast of Pan, Feast of Torches, Feast of Waxing Light, Oimelc, and Brigit's Day. Imbolc celebrates the first stirrings of spring and the recovery of the goddess from giving birth to the sun (the god) at Yule.

Immanent. Something that exists or remains within. It can be something inherent.

Initiation. A process whereby an individual is introduced or admitted into a group, interest, skill, or religion. A candidate of Wicca often undergoes it. Initiations can be ritual occasions and can also occur spontaneously.

Invocation. An appeal or petition to a higher power (or powers) such as the god or goddess (lord and the lady). A prayer. Invocation is actually a method of establishing conscious ties with those aspects of the goddess and god that dwell within us. In essence, then, we seemingly cause them to appear or make themselves known by becoming aware of them.

Kabbalah. The occult theosophy with rabbinical origins. It's an obscure interpretation of Hebrew scriptures with strong ritualistic overtones.

Karma. The law of karma is simply cause and effect. For every action, there is an equal reaction. It demonstrates that whatever you do will come back to you.

Kemetic Witchcraft. An attempt to exactly re-create ancient Egyptian witchcraft, usually one particular time period in ancient Egyptian history.

Labrys. A double-edged axe that symbolized the goddess in ancient Crete and is still used by some Wiccans for the same purpose. The two axe heads represent the goddess in her lunar aspect.

Law of Attraction. What you put out is what will come to you.

Left-Hand Path. Black magick, which is used to manipulate free will or cause harm.

Libations. In Wicca, an offering to the goddess and god of wine (or another beverage) blessed within the circle. Can also be used in Wicca to include the offering of whatever food was shared during the circle as well.

Lughnasadh. A Wiccan Sabbat celebrated on August 1. Also known as August Eve, Lammas, and Feast of Bread. Lughnasadh marks the first harvest, when the fruits of the earth are cut and stored for the dark winter months and the god mysteriously weakens as the days grow shorter.

Mabon. A Wiccan Sabbat occurring on or around September 21, the Autumnal Equinox. Mabon is a celebration of the second harvest, when nature prepares for winter. Mabon is a remnant of ancient harvest festivals.

Maiden. Coven's right-hand woman. A skilled individual who assists the high priest and high priestess.

Magic. Comes from the root meaning "to be able, to have power." Magic is what an entertainer does on stage—card tricks, making things disappear, sawing someone in half, etc.

Magick. Comes from the same root as *magic* but is in the realm of witches and may include spells, healing, the harnessing of psychic forces, and divination. It is the direction and application of energy. Spelled with a *k* to distinguish the belief in using the universe's energy for spiritual purposes from the magical illusions performed by entertainers.

Magick Circle. A two-dimensional circle constructed of personal power in which Wiccan rituals are usually enacted. It is created through visualization and magick. The circle completely surrounds and protects you.

Magickal Correspondence. Items, objects, days, colors, moon phases, oils, angels, and herbs used in rituals that match the intent of the celebration or ceremony.

Magick Witchcraft Temple. A special room (or outdoor location) where witches perform their magic. It is also a storage place for candles, textbooks, and other equipment. On the floor are painted two concentric magick circles.

Magnus. A magician or sorcerer.

Manifesting Magick. Using one's will to make something happen.

Meditation. Reflection, contemplation—turning inward toward self, or outward toward deity or nature. A quiet time in which the practitioner may either dwell upon particular thoughts or symbols or allow them to come unbidden.

Medium. A person who has the ability to become a middle ground between our world and the world of the dead, therefore allowing the dead to speak through him or her.

Metaphysical. Events that occur beyond physical explanations.

Midsummer. The summer solstice, and Wiccan festival, occurring on or near June 21. Midsummer marks the time of the year when the sun (the god) is symbolically at the height of his powers.

Mirror Book. A witch's personal account of his or her growth and evolution as a witch.

Neopagan. "New Pagan." A member or follower of one of the newly formed pagan religions now spreading throughout the world. All Wiccans are pagans, but not all pagans are Wiccans.

Neopaganism. It basically means a system of worshiping nature and the gods of nature.

Numerology. The metaphysical science of numbers. It is supposed to help people discover who they are, where they're going, and who they will become.

Occult. A set of mostly unrelated divination and/or spirtual practices which appear to tap into forces that have not been explained by science, and which are not conventional practices seen in traditional religions.

Occultism. The belief in practices like alchemy, astrology, divination, and magick that are all based on "hidden knowledge" about the universe and its mystifying forces. People who practice the occult try to tap into this invisible knowledge to bring about whatever effects they wish for.

Old Ones. A Wiccan term sometimes used to encompass all aspects of the goddess and god.

Oracle. A person of great knowledge who speaks the wisdom of spirit.

Ordains. A set of practical, spiritual, and coven laws that govern those involved in Wicca.

Ostara. Occurs around March 21 at the spring equinox. Ostara marks the beginning of true, astronomical spring, when snow and ice make way for green. As such, Ostara is a fire and fertility Sabbat, celebrating the return of the sun, the god, and the fertility of the earth (the goddess).

Otherworld. The world where spirits abide, waiting to be reborn.

Ouija. A board that has the letters, numbers, and other signs written on it and that is used together with a planchette to seek messages of spiritualistic or telepathic origin.

Pagan. Derived from the Latin *paganus,* meaning *peasant* or *hut dweller.* Pagan religions are natural religions both in origin and in mode of expressions as opposed to artificially created ideological religions. Pagan is also a general term for magick embracing religions, such as Wicca, Druid, and Shaman. Sometimes interchangeably with NeoPagan.

Paganism. In general, this term is accepted as an umbrella term for Wiccans, Shamans, Druids, the craft, and an assortment of others whose beliefs are polytheistic, nature-oriented, and in some way focus on magick.

Palmistry. The art of reading the hands. From a person's hands you can supposedly learn a lot about them physically, mentally, and emotionally. Allegedly a hand will also tell you about a person's past, present, and future.

Pantheon. The collection of all the deities from one culture. It can also be a temple that has been dedicated to all of the gods.

Pentacle. A ritual object (usually a circular piece of wood, metal, clay, etc.) upon which a five-pointed star (pentagram) is inscribed, painted, or engraved, point up, with a circle around the star. It represents the earth, air, fire, water, and spirit of the human, encompassed by the never-ending love (circle) of spirit. The words *pentacle* and *pentagram* are not interchangeable.

Pentagram. The basic interlaced five-pointed star, visualized with one point upward. The pentagram represents the five senses, elements (earth, air, fire, water, and akasha), the hand, and the human body. It is a symbol of power and is a protective symbol known to have been in use since the days of old Babylon. Today it is frequently associated with Wicca.

Personal Altar. A surface designated by a witch to represent his or her place of power.

Personal Power. That energy which sustains our bodies. It originates within the goddess and god. We first absorb it from our biological mother within the womb, and later from food, water, the moon and sun, and other natural objects. We release it during movement, exercise, sex, conception, and childbirth. Magick is a movement of personal power for a specific goal.

Planetary Hours. A system of hourly division associated with planetary energies.

Poppet. A magickal doll. A witch concentrates on the magick he or she wants to do while making a poppet. Related to the word *puppet*.

Potion. A liquid contrived with magickal components and through magickal processes to produce a specific result.

Power. The subtle energy that comes from the mind. In Germany it is called "vril" and in India "prana." Those who practice martial arts call it "chi."

Power/lineage. Energy and history passed from one person to another.

Psychic Mind. The subconscious or unconscious mind, in which people allegedly receive psychic impressions. The psychic mind is at work when people sleep, dream, and meditate. It is the direct link with the divine, and with the larger, nonphysical world around us.

Psychism. The act of being consciously psychic, in which the psychic mind and conscious mind are linked and working in harmony. Also known as psychic awareness.

Rede. An archaic word that means "advice" or "counsel." In Wicca it is a good rule to live by. Also see *Wiccan Rede*.

Reincarnation. The belief that life and death are a cycle. After leaving this life, the soul spends time in the spirit world until it is reborn to experience various situations and perspectives. One of the doctrines of Wicca.

Ritual. Ceremony. A specific form of movement. A manipulation of objects or inner processes designed to produce desired effects. In religion, ritual is geared toward union with the divine. In magick it produces a specific state of consciousness that allows the magician to move energy toward needed goals. A spell is a magick ritual.

Ritual Consciousness. A specific, alternate state of awareness necessary to the successful practice of magick. The magician achieves this consciousness through the use of visualization and ritual. It is an attunement of the conscious mind with the psychic mind, a state in which the magician senses energies, gives them purpose, and releases them toward the magick goal. It is heightening of the senses, an expanded awareness of the nonphysical world, a linking with nature and with the forces behind all conceptions of deity.

Ritual Purification. The practice of cleansing the body and mind prior to performing a ritual.

Runes. They are basically old alphabets that were used by the ancient Germans, Scandinavians, and Anglo-Saxons. Each letter in the runic alphabet also has magickal and symbolic meaning. These symbols are once again widely being used in magick and divination.

Sabbat. A Wiccan holiday.

Sacred Space. Witches will often create a "sacred space" where they can work their magick. This entails putting up a protective sphere of energy (often called a magick circle). The magick circle holds energy in place and keeps negative influences outside. When the work is finished, the sacred space is dismissed.

Samhain. A Wiccan Sabbat celebrated on October 31, also known as

November Eve, Hallowmass, Halloween, Feast of Souls, Feast of the Dead, Feast of Apples. Samhain marks the symbolic death of the sun god and his passing into the "land of the young," where he awaits rebirth of the Mother Goddess at Yule. This Celtic word is pronounced by Wiccans as "SOW-wen" (the "sow" sounds like the first three letters in sour).

Sanskrit. The ancient language of India.

Scry. To gaze at or into an object (a quartz crystal sphere, pool of water, reflections, a candle flame) to still the conscious mind in order to contact the psychic mind. This practice allows the scryer to become aware of events prior to their actual occurrence, as well as to perceive past or present events through ways other than the five senses. A form of divination.

Shaman. A medicine man or priest from a non-technological culture. Shamans engage in a lot of different activities, including astral projection, fasting, sleep deprivation, and drugs to help themselves attain altered states of consciousness.

Shrine. A sacred place that holds a collection of objects representing deity.

Sigil. A magickal sign, seal, or image. Used for everything from inscribing magick tools to letter writing to empowering a poppet.

Simple Feast. A ritual meal shared with the goddess and god.

Skyclad. Literally means "clothed by the sky" (naked), used to describe ritualistic worship without clothing.

Smudging. A ritual used whenever or wherever the need is felt to cleanse, balance, protect, or purify oneself, others, a room, one's crystals, or other specific tools. Smoke from an embering bundle of sage is used.

Solitary Witch. A witch who practices and works alone.

Spell. A magickal recipe used to affect change. It has a number of components including chanting, ritual, meditation, visualization, and magickal objects.

Spirits of the Stones. The elemental energies naturally inherent within the four directions of the earth. They are personified within the standing stones tradition as the "Spirits of the Stones," and in other Wiccan traditions as the "Lords of the Watchtowers." They are linked with the elements.

Spirit. The overall energy that runs the universe in a harmonious way. Also referred to as the lord and lady—the feminine and masculine side of God.

Sorcery. The use of magick accessible to ordinary people; such as setting out offerings to helpful spirits or using charms.

Summerland. Wiccan version of heaven. Where spirits go after death to rest and reflect in the company of the god and goddess, and to decide how they are going to reincarnate.

Sympathy. A universal law that associates like objects with like objects.

Talisman. An object charged with personal power to attract a specific force or energy to its bearer.

Tameran Witchcraft. Any modern form of witchcraft based at least in part on ancient Egyptian witchcraft, including some forms of eclectic witchcraft and some forms of Wicca.

Taoism. A Chinese religion/philosophy with several similarities to the craft—especially the emphasis on spiritual polarity. In Taoism this is conceived by the yin and yang; in Wicca it's the goddess and god; as well as the interconnectedness of all things.

Tarot Cards. A divination tool that people have used for centuries.

Tarot Spread. The pattern in which the cards are laid out when doing a reading. There are a lot of different spreads that can be used.

Telekinesis. The moving of a stationary object—without touching it—by using the power of the mind. It's a direct influence of mind over matter, causing movement without demonstrating physical energy or force.

Temple Summoner. Coven's right-hand man. A skilled individual who assists the High Priest and High Priestess.

Theban Script. A form of writing that helps focus a witch's energy and send it into the object that you are inscribing.

Third Eye. One of the chakras, positioned in the center of the forehead and associated with the pineal gland. The chakra is related to the power of inner vision, both active visualization and the ability to see between the worlds.

Totem. An animal symbol or spirit that guides one throughout life.

Tradition, Wiccan. An organized, structured, specific Wiccan subgroup, which is usually initiatory, often with unique ritual practices. Many traditions have their own Books of Shadows, and usually recognize members of other traditions as Wiccan. Most traditions are composed of a number of covens as well as solitary practitioners.

Underworld. The opposite of the living. According to mythology, it was formally earth but then came under the rule of Hades, the Greek god of the dead.

Visualization. The process of forming mental images. Magickal visualization consists of forming images of needed goals during ritual. Visualization is also used to direct personal power and natural energies for various purposes during magick, including charging and forming the magick circle. It is a function of the conscious mind. The practice of training your mind to "see" an object in your thoughts to bring it to you on the physical plane.

Voodoo. A charm that is thought to embody magickal powers or to bewitch by, or as if by, a voodoo. It is also a religious cult practiced mainly in Caribbean countries—especially Haiti—and involves animistic deities.

Wand. A tool made of wood or metal used to cast or direct energy.

Wards. Mystical energy patterns designed to safeguard a person or area from negative influences. They are often drawn in the air at the four quarters of a sacred space to enforce the protective energy.

Warlock. Another word for traitor. It is not used to describe a male witch. A male witch is also called a witch or a Wiccan.

Watchtowers. Sometimes referred to as the "Guardians of the Watchtowers," they are powerful entities associated with the four elements and the four directions. They are said to be very powerful, and some witches view them as archangels.

White-Handled Knife. A normal cutting knife with a sharp blade and a white handle. It is used within Wicca to cut herbs and fruits, to slice bread during the simple feast, and for other functions but never for sacrifice. Sometimes called the "bolline."

White Witchcraft. "Positive" witchcraft, associated with goodness, not evil.

Wicca. From the Anglo-Saxon word *wicce*, which means to shape or bend nature to one's service. A loosely connected group of about 150 modern Western witchcraft religions. It is also known as the practice of folk magick (the magick of the people). It is a contemporary pagan religion with spiritual roots in the earliest expressions of reverence of nature. Some of its major identifying motifs are: reverence for the goddess and god, acceptance of reincarnation and magic, ritual observance of astronomical and agricultural phenomena, and the creation and use of spheroid temples for ritual purposes.

Wiccan Rede. The ethic by which Wiccans live. The Rede can be summarized by the following eight-word statement: "An ye harm none, do what ye will." It is the code by which all Wiccans must adhere.

Widdershins. A counter-clockwise motion in the Wiccan dance that is thought to draw energy with negative qualities. It is usually used in the Northern Hemisphere for negative magical purposes, or for dispersing negative energies or conditions such as disease. Southern Hemisphere Wiccans may use widdershins motions for exactly the opposite purposes, namely, for positive ends. In either case, widdershins and deosil motions are symbolic; only strict, closed-minded traditionalists believe that accidentally walking around the altar backward, for instance, will raise negativity. Widdershins motions are still shunned by the majority of Wiccans, though some use it while, for instance, dispersing the magick circle at the end of a rite.

Witch. Someone who seeks to control the forces within him- or herself—that make life possible in order to live wisely and well without harm to others and in harmony with nature. In ancient times, a practitioner of the remnants of pre-Christian folk magick, particularly that kind related to herbs, stones, wells, and rivers. One who practices witchcraft.

Witchcraft. The craft of the witch—magic or sorcery—especially magic utilizing personal power in conjunction with the energies within stones, herbs, colors, and other natural objects. However, some followers of Wicca use this word to denote their religion. The term is used in many different ways in different places and times.

Witches' Pyramid. A creed and structure of learning that witches follow. It can be summarized as: to know, to dare, to will, and to be silent.

Wortcunning. The art of growing and using herbs for magickal and healing purposes.

Wyrt. The Old English word for "plant" or "herb."

Yin and Yang. They are archetypal opposites—the negative, passive, and female versus the positive, active, and male. From Chinese Taoist philosophy.

Yule. A Wiccan Sabbat celebrated on or about December 21, marking the rebirth of the sun god from the earth goddess. Yule occurs at the winter solstice.

Note: Most of these definitions come from Wiccan and witchcraft literature/sources.

WICCAN HOLIDAYS AND THE WHEEL OF THE YEAR

Greater Sabbats

- Samhain (Halloween): October 31
- Beltane (Rudemas): April 30th/May 1
- Imbolc (Candlemas): February 2
- Lughnasadh (Lammas): July 30/August 1

Lesser Sabbats

- Winter Solstice (Yule): December 21/22
- Spring Equinox (Ostara): March 21/22
- Summer Solstice (Midsummer Eve): June 21/22
- Autumn Equinox (Mabon): September 21/ 22

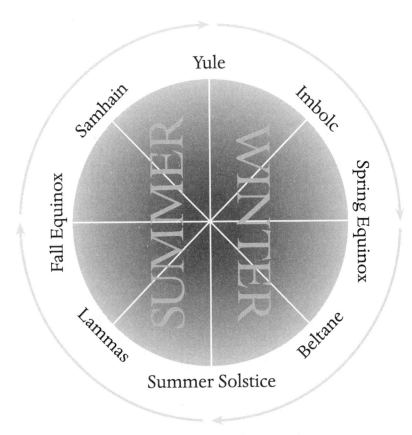

WHEEL OF THE YEAR

SYMBOLS

Pentagram. A five-pointed star, with the sides interwoven. It has also been called the Endless Knot because it can be drawn with a single line. Generally, the top point represents the spirit (Akasha) and the other points represent wind, fire, earth, and water—substances that are crucial to all life. It has become the symbol of witchcraft, Wicca, and neopaganism.

Some witches also view the five points as representing the three aspects of the goddess—maiden, mother, and crone, and the two aspects of the god—dark and light.

Pentacle. A pentagram with a circle drawn around it.

Sacred Spirals. Represents the dance of divine energy within the world of a witch. Drawn clockwise, the sacred spiral brings things inward; drawn counterclockwise, the spiral pushes negative energies away. The spiral also signifies the ancient journey within.

Equal-Armed Cross. Represents another powerful magickal symbol. This cross stands for many ideals—the four seasons, the four directions, the four archangels, the four winds, and the four quarters of the magick circle. Drawn in the air or on paper from top to bottom and right to left with the right hand, the symbol represents healing energies. Drawn from top to bottom and left to right with the left hand signifies banishing negative energies. A witch also employs the equal-armed cross to "seal" a magickal working so that negative energies cannot reverse the positive efforts of the magickal person.

 **Goddess symbol.** The symbol of the goddess (full moon in the middle flanked by crescent moons) signifies the feminine aspect of spirit, women's mysteries, and the healing of the divine. Witches use this symbol to connect with the divine feminine and wear the image to show their faith in the Lady.

CONTACT INFORMATION

For more information on how to purchase audio and video resources, CDs, drum stuff, and other books by Steve Russo, as well as information on the *Real Answers* and *Life on the Edge—Live!* radio programs, the *Real Answers* TV show, citywide evangelistic events, or public school assemblies, please contact:

Real Answers with Steve Russo
P.O. Box 1549
Ontario, CA 91762
(909) 466-7060
FAX (909) 466-7056
E-mail: Russoteam@realanswers.com

You can also visit our web sites at:

www.realanswers.com
or
www.steverusso.com